Writing the Private Eye Novel
A Handbook by
The Private Eye Writers of America

WRITING THE
PRIVATE EYE NOVEL

A HANDBOOK BY
The Private Eye
Writers of America

EDITED BY
Robert J. Randisi

WRITER'S DIGEST BOOKS
CINCINNATI, OHIO

This hardcover edition of *Writing the Private Eye Novel* features a "self-jacket" that eliminates the need for a separate dust jacket. It provides sturdy protection for your book while it saves paper, trees and energy.

Other fine Writer's Digest Books are available from your local bookstore or direct from the publisher.

01   00   99   98   97   5   4   3   2   1

Library of Congress Cataloging-in-Publication Data

Writing the private eye novel / edited by Robert J. Randisi.—1st ed.
    p.   cm.
Copyright by: The Private Eye Writers of America.
Includes index.
ISBN 0-89879-767-5 (hardcover : alk. paper)
    1. Detective and mystery stories—Authorship. 2 Fiction—Technique. 3. Creative writing. I. Randisi, Robert J. II. Private Eye Writers of America.
PN3377.5.D4W74   1997
808.3'872—dc21   97-13699
                                                                          CIP

Cover illustration by Harry Bliss
Edited by Robert J. Randisi
Interior designed by Brian Roeth
Cover designed by Angela Lennert Wilcox

TABLE OF CONTENTS

INTRODUCTION

Whenever I teach a course—whether a one-day, three-day, week-long or even longer course—my first announcement to the assembled "students" is usually along the lines: "If any of you have come here to learn to write, get up and leave now."

You see, I believe that you cannot be taught to "write." You can be taught grammar and punctuation, but you cannot be taught to be a writer. That has to come from within. Whether published or unpublished, the first step to being a writer is to admit that you are. Too many beginning writers think that you have to be published to be a writer. Not so. I started writing when I was fifteen years old, and even though I did not sell my first short story until I was twenty-three—and my first novel until I was twenty-nine—I was already a writer.

So, if you're reading this, as far as I'm concerned, you are a writer. (If only someone had said that to me when I was starting out—"You are a writer." It's a bit of encouragement I never got during my first ten years.)

Recently, an agent who shall go nameless—and soon, one would hope, jobless—told a writer who had published poetry and short stories, audio stories and radio scripts, and who was a produced playwright—albeit off-off-off Broadway—that she was not a writer because she did not have a book published. Any agent who spouts this kind of drivel should be horse-whipped.

I believe it is the duty of people in the so-called writing business—which some people have been known to call the publishing business, depending on which end you're on—to encourage writers to write, not to tell them they're not writers because they don't write a certain type of thing.

I mentioned earlier that I have taught writing courses. It would be more accurate to say that I have lectured on writing certain kinds of fiction. When I do this I first want to encourage the people in the room—who are writers and don't need me to tell them that—to keep writing. Secondly, I try to explain how to write a certain kind of story. My expertise, for the most part, has been in the private eye genre for the past thirty years. (No, I'm not that old. Remember I said that I have been a writer since I was fifteen.)

Which brings us to the point of this book. The professionals represented herein are sharing with you their expertise on certain aspects of writing private eye—hereinafter referred to as PI—fiction. They are not here to teach you how to write. If you have this book in your hands we expect that you already know how to do that. What we are going to do is try to give you some insight into what it takes to write PI fiction.

THE AUTHORS

Parnell Hall is the current president of the Private Eye Writers of America. In "Writing the Private Eye Novel" he gives you some insight into what it took for him to write his first PI novel, *Detective*. This complements nicely Christine Matthews's tale of writing her first PI short story after having written over twenty horror short stories under her *real* name—which we are not giving away here. Her piece is called "I Can Do That!" and if you find a copy of *Deadly Allies II* and read "Gentle Insanities" you'll find out that she is right.

Parnell, author of the Stanley Hastings series, also examines for you his method of writing humorous PI novels.

Jeremiah Healy is the creator of one of the most popular PI characters of recent years, John Francis Cuddy. Cuddy has appeared in eleven novels from *Blunt Darts* through *Invasion of Privacy*. This makes Jerry highly qualified to write his piece, "Developing a Series Character." He is also a past president of PWA, and a past winner of the Shamus Award.

Max Allan Collins has been nominated for more Shamus Awards than I can count. So far, he has won two of them for Best PI Novel, with *True Detective* and *Stolen Away*, two novels in his Nate Heller series. The Heller books are set in the thirties, forties and fifties, and Max Collins was an early practitioner of a form that has since become very popular, the History Mystery. He demonstrates the form in "Private Eye Witness." He will also offer a short lesson on "Writing for the Comics."

Jan Grape writes a successful series of short stories about her Austin, Texas-based PIs Jenny Gordon and C.J. Gunn. In "A Trip Into the Hinterlands" she shows you how to bring your setting to life, virtually making it a character in your stories.

Jerry Keneally is an actual private detective in San Francisco, and he brings reality to his novels about PI Nick Polo. He is eminently qualified to discuss how to "Write What You Know and Fake the Rest." Jerry is also past vice-president of PWA.

Three past presidents of PWA offer invaluable instruction and suggestion in "Putting Yourself on the Page," by Les Roberts; "A Personal Journal," by Sue Grafton; and "Short and Shamus," by John Lutz. Les is a past Shamus nominee, and winner of the first PWA/St. Martin's Press First Private Eye Novel contest back in 1987—some eleven books ago. Both Sue Grafton and John Lutz have won Shamus Awards, Sue three times for Best PI Novel and John twice, once for Best Novel and once for Best PI Short Story.

Loren D. Estleman, author of the Amos Walker series, has often commented on how long and boring the wrap-up of some books can be, and so he offers "And the Murderer Is . . . ," a way to end your book without benefit of a long-winded explanation. Loren is a three-time winner of the Shamus Award.

Wendi Lee offers her thoughts on two fascinating subjects, "The Trans-Gender Writer," that is, men writing from a female point of view and vice-versa, and "Crossing Over," writing in more than one genre. Wendi writes the Angela Matelli PI series, as well as the Jefferson Birch western PI series.

Catherine Dain, a two-time Shamus nominee for Best Paperback Western with books in her Freddy O'Neal series, talks a bit about writing the female PI in the nineties, and Ed Gorman has two offerings, one about the importance of reading if you want to be a writer, and another about "The Care and Feeding of a PI Series." Ed has been nominated for almost every major genre award available, including the Edgar, the Shamus, the Spur and the Bram Stoker. He is a past Shamus winner.

Gar Anthony Haywood has won two Shamus awards, one for Best First PI Novel and most recently for Best PI Short Story. Gar has also recently joined the ranks of television writers, working on the series *New York Undercover*. He demonstrates for us the differences between writing for print and for TV.

And what would a book like this be without Lawrence Block? Mr. Block has graciously allowed us to reprint some articles that will be very helpful to beginning PI writers.

I think you can see that the quality of our "faculty" in PWA's *Writing the PI Novel* is extraordinary, and the value of the information contained herein is immeasurable.

ABOUT THE PWA

A bit of history before we close. I founded the Private Eye Writers of America in 1981. The first Shamus Awards were presented in 1982, and are presented each year in the categories of Best PI Novel, Best First PI Novel, Best PI Short Story and Best Paperback PI Novel. There is also a Life Achievement Award called the "Eye," which has been presented to the likes of Ross Macdonald, Mickey Spillane, Bill Pronzini and Marcia Muller.

Past presidents include Bill Pronzini, Lawrence Block, Sue Grafton, Jeremiah Healy and Parnell Hall.

For information about joining as either an Active or an Associate Member write to: Martha Derickson, Membership Chair, 407 W. Third St., Moorestown, NJ 08057.

Now it's time to take your lessons from the best PI writers in the business. Pay close attention. There will be a test afterwards—the first time you submit your work to an editor for publication. We hope you pass.

ROBERT J. RANDISI
ST. LOUIS, MISSOURI

GETTING STARTED

Writing the Private Eye Novel

Parnell Hall

I hesitate to give anyone advice on how to write a PI novel, because it is my personal belief that writing cannot be taught. I took a creative writing course in college, and the only thing I ever learned was that the word *past* refers only to time and not to distance. You can't, for instance, say the man walked past the drug store. You can say he passed it, but not that he went past it. Since this is the only thing I learned in college, I try to include at least one incorrect usage of *past* in every book I write. (If sharp-eyed readers would care to point out the books in which I fail to do so, please feel free.)

At any rate, my view is that writing is a talent that cannot be taught—basically, if you don't have it going in, you're not going to have it coming out.

One might ask, if that's my view, why am I writing this article? Well, I happen to be president of the Private Eye Writers of America. As such, my opinion should certainly be included in this volume. Also, I should be an inspiration to any aspiring private eye writer—if a person like me can get to be president of PWA, clearly there is hope for anyone.

And, while I believe writing cannot be *taught*, I believe it can be *learned*. In other words, it is possible for each aspiring writer to find something that is useful just to them.

My own personal experience is a case in point. I wrote my first mystery novel in the mid-eighties. I hadn't written one until then because I didn't think I could. Then I read *Looking For Rachel Wallace*, by Robert B. Parker. Up till then I'd only read Erle Stanley Gardner and Agatha Christie, and I thought that was how you had to do it. You either had a dramatic courtroom revelation, or you had a number of suspects and clues, and came up with a surprising but totally logical and fair solution. I didn't feel I could do either of these things, which is why I never wrote a mystery.

THE WAY THE WORDS SOUND

Looking for Rachel Wallace took my head off. It has virtually no plot—Spenser bodyguards a woman, she's kidnapped, he pokes around some, decides somewhat arbitrarily which of the suspects did it, walks out to the guy's house and rescues her. Pretty dull book, right? Wrong. It is terrific. And it made me think, hmmm, maybe I could do this after all.

Shortly after that I saw Parker interviewed on TV. He was asked, "Why do you think people like your books?" I thought, poor Bob, what can he say but something like, "I think they like Spenser because although he's a macho figure, he's also an intellectual and a gourmet cook." He didn't. He said, "I think they like the way the words sound." The interviewer blinked and said, "Huh?" and Parker said, "Yes. If the words sound good, people enjoy reading them, and I think people like my books because they like the way the words sound." I must confess, I felt like the interviewer—Bob, give me a break, no one reads this stuff out loud. Then I read *Rachel Wallace* again and realized, damn, he's right, I like the way these words sound.

When I started my first book, *Detective*, a few months later, I had no idea what the plot was; I just took a premise and started writing. But the one thing I was concerned with was that I wanted it to sound good. That book got excellent reviews and an Edgar and a Shamus nomination. I feel I owe those reviews and nominations to Robert B. Parker, and I believe they reflect the fact that people liked the way the words sounded.

I realize if I were to relate this to Robert B. Parker, he'd probably say, "Gee, Parnell, couldn't you tell I was putting the guy on?" But it doesn't matter. The fact is, it helped me. Even though it will probably not help you, because everybody's an individual, and everybody's got to do it their own way. The point is, if I can find something that helped me, you can find something that will help you. Even if it's something that's special to you that wouldn't help anybody else. So I offer up my own experiences, in the hope that some small part of them will strike a chord with someone somewhere.

THROW A MURDER AT 'EM

One thing that helped me write a PI novel was working two years as a private detective. Which, believe me, is not as glamorous as it sounds. On TV, or in the movies, when they want to show how boring private detective work is, they show the PI sitting in his car all night drinking coffee and waiting for some guy's wife to come out so he can tail her to a motel. But that's not boring. That's exciting. That's surveillance. I interviewed accident victims and photographed cracks in the sidewalk. I worked for a detective agency that serviced negligence lawyers, the kind that advertise on TV. When someone got injured they would call the law firm, who would call the detective agency, who would send me out to investigate. I would interview the prospective clients, sign them to a retainer and photograph the broken arm or leg and the scene of the accident, as I say, usually a crack in the sidewalk. I didn't carry a gun, I carried a camera, and any resemblance between me and a TV detective was entirely coincidental and not to be inferred.

I had hoped to find inspiration in my detective work, something to write about. But it did not take me long to learn that real detective work was so excruciatingly dull that there was nothing to write about at all.

So I wrote about that.

I started some dialogue running. The client and the detective. The classic scene. The detective is in his office, and the client has come to him for help. In this case, the man Albrect tells a story of how he ran up gambling debts, and then to pay them off, got involved with drug smugglers and wound up ripping off part of their cocaine shipment and replacing it with milk sugar, only now they are onto him and want to kill him.

This is where the detective says, "There, there, citizen. You've been a damn fool, but I'll help you," straps on his gun, and goes out to deal with the bad guys.

But my guy, Stanley Hastings, says, "Are you kidding me? I don't have a gun, I have a camera. I take pictures of cracks in the sidewalk."

Albrect is subsequently killed. Stanley feels terrible, and spends the rest of the book trying to make up for the fact that he couldn't help him because he wasn't a real detective.

Okay, you can see where I got my character. Basically, he's just me, a poor schmuck doing the job I did.

Where did I get my plot? I just took that guy and threw a murder at him.

Essentially.

But where did the scene in the office come from? The first scene, where Stanley can't help the man and sends him away?

Actually, I had no idea when I wrote it, and didn't find out until years later when I was on a panel about getting your first novel published, and I had to stop and analyze what I had done. So here's where that first scene came from.

Before I was a writer, I was an actor, and a few years back I had a part in a movie. I played a cop, and I had a scene where I found a body down by the Hudson River. The movie was working wardrobe out of a brownstone in Chelsea, so early in the morning I went there, got into costume and makeup, and went out and waited on the sidewalk for the teamster to show up and drive me to the set.

And while I was standing there a man ran up to me and said, "You've got to help me, my girlfriend's been kidnapped."

You must understand. I was not a successful actor, I didn't work very often, and I was totally absorbed in the part I was about to play. So, not thinking, I said the very worst thing I could have said to this man.

"I'm not a cop."

You cannot believe the look on that man's face. It wasn't

just that I was refusing to help him. But I was standing there, *in uniform*, telling him I wasn't a cop. He just couldn't believe I could do that. To lie to him like that, such an obvious boldfaced lie. Shattering his illusions. After a moment, he cursed at me, and ran off down the street.

I had no way of knowing it, but that's the scene I was recreating when I wrote my first book. Stanley Hastings, in his detective's office, shattering Albrect's illusions by telling him he wasn't a detective, at least Albrect's idea of a detective, which is pretty much everyone's idea of a detective, which is the type you see on TV.

So there's a helpful hint. Everything is grist for the mill. Use what you know. Even if you don't know you're using it.

The converse is also true.

DON'T USE WHAT YOU DON'T KNOW

I hate research and do as little of it as possible. My two years as a private detective could count as research, but it wasn't. It was a job. Having had the experience, it now fits into the category of things I know. Acting and screenwriting also fall into that category.

But what about things I don't know?

Well, let me give you an example.

In my first novel, *Detective*, there's a scene where Stanley calls on a man who is a modern day gentleman jewel thief, and has a house filled with priceless art objects that he has stolen. I had a big problem the minute Stanley walked into the house. I know nothing about art, and didn't know how to describe the scene, and Stanley's narrative ground to a dead halt.

Like it or not, I was going to have to do some research.

I stopped writing, tried to figure out what I could do. Who did I know in the art field? Were there any art books in the house? Should I go to the library at Columbia University? Did I know anyone who would know anyone (who would know anyone . . .) in the art department? Where in the world could I possibly get enough information just to get through this scene?

That's when it hit me. Wait a minute. Why am I being so pompous and pretentious? I'm writing a first person narrative. Why does my narrator have to be brighter than I am?

So I had Stanley Hastings walk into the house, look around, say, "Boy, I don't know anything about art, but it sure looked good to me," and I'm on to the next scene.

Was that cheating the reader? It depends on where you sit. My opinion is, if I really wanted to bother, I could do an adequate enough job to fake a knowledge of art I do not in fact have. But in my opinion, that would be cheating the reader. While I could get by, I could not become proficient enough to offer those extra insights that make a subject fascinating.

OUTLINING VS. WRITING

The main thing about writing a detective story is how to begin. There are many schools of thought. Warren Murphy, for instance, is of the opinion that you shouldn't write a word until you have outlined the entire story from beginning to end, so you know exactly where you're going. He feels that if you don't do this, halfway through the book you'll get lost and not know what to do. So you'll stop, go back, work on what you've done, write your Edgar acceptance speech, and you will never finish the book.

Far be it for me to argue with a man who has written over a hundred books. Warren's argument is basically sound. Ninety percent of the time he'd probably be right.

I fall into the other 10 percent.

I never plot at all, just pick a premise and start going. I wrote a book called *Favor*, in which I sent Stanley to Atlantic City, had him following people around, and by the time I was halfway through the book two people were dead and I had no idea who killed them or why.

SERIAL CRIMES

In any event, if you set out to write a private eye novel, you should make it the start of a series. Because that's what every publisher wants. I didn't know that when I wrote my first book. I was just happy to have written it. But that was the very first question the first agent I gave it to asked me: "Is it a series character?"

I said, "No, it's completely self-contained. The protagonist is in conflict, he goes through a character change and resolves." He said, "That's too bad. All they're buying these days are series characters."

So when the next agent asked me if it was a series character, I said, "Absolutely, I'm working on a sequel."

One of the problems of writing a private eye series is coming up with new ideas and keeping the material fresh. No matter how careful you are, there is always the danger of repeating yourself. After all, if you are working with the same private eye in the same city with the same supporting characters, and every case is a murder investigation, the odds of similarities cropping up in your books are actually rather high.

I learned this early on in my series. I was in my fourth book, *Strangler*. In the beginning of the book I had Stanley running around New York City signing up accident victims for the negligence lawyer he worked for. I wrote a scene where he goes to an apartment in Harlem to interview a prospective client, and he finds a black man who's been strangled. He calls the police and they come, and the sergeant asks him what happened. He's explaining that the law office beeped him and sent him to this address and he walked in and found the client strangled.

Suddenly I realized I'd written the exact same scene in my second book, *Murder*: Stanley, in an apartment in Harlem, explaining to the police how he got beeped, sent over and found the client, a black man, lying there dead.

I was horrified. I mean, there I was, four books into the series, totally out of ideas on the one hand, and so oblivious on the other that I could go ahead and write identical scenes in two books and not even realize I was doing it.

So I thought, what do I do now? Do I have to start over? Do I have to rewrite the scene? Exchange the character and the setting? Make the victim a white man in Queens? Would that make any difference? Could I have someone else find the body and call the cops? No, that wouldn't work—Stanley finding the body was the premise of the book.

Then I said, no, I have to have this happen, so let's assume that this happened and work with it. That being the case, how would Stanley react?

Stanley being Stanley, I had him think, "Wow. *Déjà vu.* Isn't that amazing. I've done this exact same thing before."

So, rather than try to hide the similarity, I point it out. And it becomes a major plot point. Later in the book, the sergeant calls Stanley into his office and says, "I've discovered a clue. A similarity between this case and a case last year. Another black man in Harlem you called on who was also murdered. The two cases are very similar, and I think what we are dealing with here is a serial killer."

Stanley is astounded. He knows the two crimes are totally unrelated. In the other case, the man he called on wasn't a client. Stanley had just told the police he was because otherwise he had no reason for calling on him, and he needed to get out of a jam. But he can't tell the homicide investigator that. And he can't say, "Don't be silly, that was in another book." No, he has to deal with it, frustrating as that is for him. And it becomes another plot complication.

So that's basically what I do. I go where the story leads me. And if I run into trouble, well, that creates plot.

I have to issue a disclaimer here. Describing the way I write makes it sound as if my books are the most illogical, disjointed stories ever written. In my defense, I would like to point out that Jon L. Breen, reviewing my series in *Ellery Queen's Mystery Magazine* says, "Stanley's cases have going for them some of the deftest and trickiest puzzle-plotting in the field today."

I appreciate that, because that is my intention, and that is how the books turn out, even though they do not come from a pre-plotted outline.

But again, I issue the warning. This works for me. It

probably will not for you. I strongly recommend Warren Murphy's idea of working from a plot outline and knowing where you're going.

STRETCH CREDULITY

Once you get started, a main concern is whether your story is believable. Are there plot holes, are there inconsistencies, and is your story contrived? This is one thing editors are quick to pounce on. I can recall reading editing notes such as, "Is it really believable that Stanley wouldn't follow the bad guy up to the second floor, but would wait for him outside?" or "It is clear that for the plot you need Stanley in motel unit twelve, but if, as you describe, the motel is virtually empty, why would he not rent a unit closer to the road?" While I am willing to fix such things, in most cases I don't think it is particularly important.

Don't get me wrong. I don't set out to write unbelievable situations or plots that stretch credulity. And I certainly wouldn't want to write a physical impossibility. On the other hand, I don't spend a lot of time worrying about whether a particular idea, motivation or course of action is totally logical, because in my humble opinion, in most cases it doesn't really matter.

Let me give you one of my favorite examples, from the movie *North by Northwest*. This is not a bad movie. It is a good one, in fact a classic, four-star Hitchcock. In it, you will recall, Cary Grant has been framed for murder at the U.N., and now he is escaping from New York by train. He hides in a sleeping compartment occupied by Eva Marie Saint, but she is presumably in league with the bad guys. After Grant is asleep, she sends a note to their car saying, "What should I do with him in the morning?"

Very good question.

Well, since they think he is a government agent and want him dead—in fact, they have been trying to kill him for the entire movie—and since he is now completely in their power, shoot him and throw his body off the train sounds good to me. This is simple, easy and effective and would probably work.

But, no, they have a better idea.

Let's send him out in the middle of a cornfield and try to run him over with an airplane.

Oh, dear.

There it is, the stupidest, most illogical contrivance in the world.

But does it bother anyone?

Not only does it not bother anyone, but anytime you mention the movie *North by Northwest*, one of the first things everyone remembers is that great crop dusting scene.

Because it is great. You have the crossroads. With Cary Grant on the one side. And the old man on the other. And the plane in the distance. And the old man saying, "Funny. That plane's dustin' crops where there ain't no crops."

Simply wonderful.

Except for the fact it makes no sense at all.

So my theory is, if what you write is lively and entertaining, people won't notice any of the minor plot inconsistencies. They will be enjoying what they are reading too much to care.

On the other hand, if you keep adding paragraph after paragraph to try to explain each and every little plot point and justify why you wrote it, your book becomes slow and stodgy. Instead of zipping right through the plot inconsistencies, your reader will notice every single one.

THROUGH WHOSE EYES?

One last consideration—should you write a first person narrative or in the third person omniscient? I do both. My Stanley Hastings private eye novels are first person narratives. My Steve Winslow courtroom dramas, written under the pseudonym J.P. Hailey, are third person omniscient. There are advantages in both.

The advantages of the third person is that you can go anywhere, so you can jump around from scene to scene, as in a movie script. Indeed, my first Steve Winslow novel, *The Baxter Trust*, I originally wrote as a screenplay. I adapted it as a novel after I got published. And the third person omniscient is useful in the courtroom series, because I like to intercut scenes and show what both the prosecution and the defense are doing. And it's fun to get inside the prosecutor's head and see what he's thinking.

You'll notice that most private eye novels are first person narratives. I suppose this comes from the tradition of the private eye being a loner, walking the mean streets. And you want to identify with the character, stay with the character, feel what the character feels, empathize, fantasize, be the hero, save the day.

I have another reason. As I've indicated, I'm rather lazy about research. If you write a first person narrative, you see everything through the eyes of your narrator, so you need only know what your narrator knows. If you write in the first person, and your protagonist isn't very bright, you don't have to do any research at all.

On the other hand, the problem with the third person omniscient is, if you don't know anything, it's hard to be omniscient.

I don't know much. But I got published by ignoring well-intentioned advice and finding my own way to write.

I advise you to ignore my advice and do the same.

The Care and Feeding of a PI Series

Ed Gorman

Writers in the mystery field are under so much pressure now to write books in series that, typically, the first book they ever write is the first book of a series, and the writer finds himself locked into writing the same book over and over, or the same character, before he knows what the hell to do—has mastered the art of writing. I don't think that it's very easy to grow doing that, and I think the author gets locked into a character conceived of by an immature writer. I think that's a big mistake.

—Lawrence Block

This is a terrible thing for a mystery writer to admit—but I don't particularly like series, not unless the writer is careful to see that each entry offers the reader (me) something new and fresh.

I also agree with the Larry Block quote above—I've seen a number of mystery bestsellers whose series caught on quickly . . . and yet who can't write very well. Can't set scenes. Can't develop character. Don't bring any life to their material outside the plot. And yet they sell and sell and sell. . . .

Now, I'd be less than truthful if I told you I don't want to be a bestseller. I certainly do.

But I wouldn't want to be a bestseller at the expense of the things I genuinely want to say. And writing twenty or thirty books about the same lovable character and her/his wacky sidekick isn't my idea of a serious writing career.

So if I feel this way, why am I wasting my time (and yours) talking about series fiction?

Because I think there are a few things you can do to keep a series reasonably fresh, something you owe both your reader and yourself.

I'd like to offer five examples of writers who have kept their series vital and exciting.

Nancy Pickard's Jenny Cain series started out as a tart but somewhat fluffy entry in a field of fluffy entries. But Nancy Pickard is, I submit, not only a first-rate writer. She's also a true artist. With the book *Marriage Is Murder*, Nancy pointed the series in an entirely different direction. In her own fetching way, Nancy decided to kick some butt. And she did it beautifully. Nancy, like few others of either the softboiled or hardboiled variety, has managed to keep the wit and weary Midwestern wisdom of her first books, but to deepen their themes and perceptions. For me, her masterpiece thus far is *Confession*. Here, a teenaged boy shows up at Jenny's claiming to be the biological son of Geoff, Jenny's husband. From that opening chapter the book dazzles the reader with turn after unexpected turn and a quality of writing rarely seen in genre fiction of any kind. Make no mistake, Nancy's as entertaining as ever. But she has turned her mysteries into real novels. This is a series that constantly surprises and rarely disappoints.

Bill Pronzini's *Nameless* books started out as somewhat routine private eye adventures. The books had great milieu and atmosphere, but the first few books showed their familiar origins. Then Bill wrote *Blowback*, which to me remains one of the best books in the series. In this one, Nameless has to get some medical tests done. The doctor thinks there's a chance Nameless, a heavy smoker, has lung cancer. Nameless has a hard time facing the weekend; he's scared and lonely. He takes on a case for the pure diversion of it. Not only is the case the most ingenious of Nameless' early career, the possibility of lung cancer forces Nameless to examine his entire life. We get to know the guy better than we know 99.8 percent of all series leads. And Pronzini continues in this "confession" style, each book, like a chapter in the larger book of Nameless's life, telling us about the man and his times. In one book, he gets a partner. In another book, Nameless and his partner split up. Nameless meets a woman . . . they break up . . . a few books later they get together again and get married and so on. The ebb and flow of real life is what Pronzini is after in these books and he gets it down very well. He also charts the history of San Francisco over the past thirty-some years, San Francisco as a somewhat volatile, working-class man sees it. There are no two books alike in the Nameless series nor, I suspect, will there ever be. There's not a hint of Dashiell Hammett, Raymond Chandler or Robert B. Parker in the Nameless books and that helps to keep them idiosyncratic and fresh.

Consider Joan Hess's Arly Hanks and Claire Malloy series. Too many critics equate humor with silliness. If a book is *too* enjoyable, there must be something wrong with it. While I prefer Hanks (the small town police chief) to Claire Malloy (owner of a smalltown bookstore), Hess proves that "light" books can be every bit as serious as "dark" ones—sometimes even more serious. Hess creates a real smalltown Arkansas world in her books, and this is what enriches her books with wit, pique, rage, loneliness and just a wee bit of envy of people whose lives seem happier. The Malloys are particularly good at describing the interior life of a middle-aged woman who genuinely loves her teenaged daughter . . . at least most of the time. Hess keeps her books fresh by keeping her situations and observations fresh. The taint of series books is to become routine. Hess works hard at never letting this happen. If you want to learn about writing "funny," study these books carefully. Hess proves that you don't need a gimmick to make each book different. Sheer good writing can get you there.

Max Allan Collins's Nate Heller series includes a brilliant concept that ensures each book will be vital and new. In each book Nathan Heller, a detective who worked in the thirties, forties and fifties, is joined with a famous mystery or famous historical person: the Lindbergh kidnapping, Bugsy Siegel, the assassination of Huey Long. Collins always gives his reader a fascinating historical tale and a first-rate mystery packed with famous people and historical moments. Very soon now, this series will bring Collins the fame he's deserved for many years.

Look at Marcia Muller's Sharon McCone series: While the early books are much better than Marcia thinks, they certainly aren't the equal of the last five or six McCones, during which, for one thing, McCone learns how to fly. This not only offered Sharon freedom, it seemed to free Marcia, too. The books became much bigger in scope, more ambitious in terms of setting and backstory, and impressive in terms of writing style and character. It was as if, after several books, Marcia found a new passion for her series character . . . and turned McCone into virtually a new series. If you want to learn the difference between a genre book and what publishers call a "big book," compare an early McCone with one of the last three. You'll be rewarded richly for your trouble.

Ed McBain's 87th Precinct series is one to study for bombastic effects, clever use of continuing characters, and perhaps the most nimble plotting mind in all of mystery fiction. *Item:* In one novel McBain solves a murder that took place several books earlier. In another novel, his continuing characters appear only briefly—the villain is the centerpiece of the book. In a more recent novel, what might have been a very routine whodunit transcends form with the use of the murder victim's diary—the haunting words of a twenty-year-old girl as she tries to describe a doomed love affair that she knows is wrong. I've rarely seen romantic love dealt with so uniquely or powerfully. In virtually every book McBain comes up with some element of character we haven't seen before. He takes the expected and surprises you with the way he changes it. In *Romance*, Fat Ollie Weeks, the racist cop McBain uses more and more frequently these days, goes to this guy's apartment and begins to interrogate him. We think this will probably be a ho-hum Q&A. On the contrary, it becomes a hilarious set piece in which the obnoxious Ollie mooches a beer off the guy. Then Ollie finds out the guy is an actor who plays action roles, and Ollie says that this surprises him because he thinks the guy is well, uh, a little on the effeminate side. Nothing personal, you understand. Then Ollie goes on to cadge another beer and insult the guy even further. None of us is ever going to match these little moments, but we should keep reading and studying him because he has a lot to teach us. One final example of McBain's genius: *Ghosts*, certainly one of his strongest books, is an urban ghost story, a troubled romance, an eerie whodunit and a forlorn portrait of a big city during holidays. It is also one of the most compellingly readable novels I've ever picked up. Anybody who wants to learn how to enliven a series should memorize both *Ghosts* and *Blood Relatives*, where the young woman's diary is featured.

One other consideration: Vary the types of mysteries you use in the series. Most mysteries are straight whodunits, but there are a number of variations—the whydunit, the howdunit (i.e., the locked room), the multiple murderers that Agatha Christie used in *Murder on the Orient Express*, and the straight suspense novel in which your hero or heroine tries to stop a crime from taking place. All these variations on the whodunit form can be used legitimately within the confines of a PI series.

I should also note here, going along with Larry Block's words, that some novels probably shouldn't be written in series form at all. There are several Ross Macdonald novels so powerful that they suffer from having a continuing protagonist. They are so overwhelming in drama and theme, in fact, that the detective Lew Archer almost gets lost entirely. He becomes more observer than participant, and as a result the novel becomes less than it might have been.

Of course, conversely, there are novels that profit from being part of a series. *The Long Goodbye* would not have been so strong if it hadn't been preceded by the other Phillip Marlowe novels. *Goodbye* functions as a coda to the earlier books and is, in a very real sense, the summing up of Marlowe's life.

What I'm really saying here, of course, is that a series is what you make it. Most, alas, gray out after two or three entries: the little old lady detective loses whatever charm she had or the nasty old private eye finally drinks so much that he dozes off (which his audience did a long time ago).

But there are exceptions to these perils, and you could be one of them if you've got the talent and determination to keep your books a pleasure to write and read.

I really do agree with what Larry Block said at the outset, though. If you're just starting out, try to write a few books of a series. You'll learn a lot, and you may even improve your series in the bargain—because you'll have more experience as a writer.

Nobody ever said it was going to be easy, did they?

PLOT AND STRUCTURE

The Deadly Cruise

Lawrence Block

There are really only three things you have to do," I heard a man say. "First of all, you have to get them on board. Then you have to make sure you keep them on the ship. And finally, you have to kill them at the end."

I thought at first that I was overhearing a declamation from *Every Boy's Guide to Piracy*, and my head swam with visions of peglegged parrots wearing eye patches and Hathaway shirts, brandishing cutlasses and leaving no swash unbuckled. But I was not tossing on the high seas, or tossing 'em back in some waterfront dive. I was at a party in Greenwich Village, and there was not a pirate in the room. (There were, however, a couple of agents, and the distinction between the two is a narrow one indeed.)

But the speaker was neither pirate nor agent. He was Donald E. Westlake, the prominent mystery novelist and occasional screenwriter, and the violent criminal activity he was advocating was strictly metaphoric, and to be perpetrated on dry land. He was talking about writing, and the intended victims were readers.

"First you've got to pipe them abroad," he explained. "You've got to hook them good and get them into the boat. Then all you have to do is provide enough shipboard activity to keep them there. Decent food, plenty to drink. Entertainment in the evenings—a juggler one night, some played-out operatic soprano the next. Remember, you've got an essentially captive audience here. They'd just as soon stay put.

"And then, at the end, you've got to kill 'em. Or the whole cruise is a failure."

THREES

For years I've watched speakers stand up in front of rooms full of writers and explain that every story has a beginning and a middle and an ending. While I've never had occasion to argue with this bit of wisdom, neither have I ever seen what good it does anyone to know it. A story has a beginning and a middle and an ending. Terrific. A person has legs, a trunk, and a head. So what? Now that we know that, what do we know?

Listening to Mr. Westlake, however, it struck me that dividing a story like Gaul into three parts might be of value in detailing what we must do to make the fiction we write satisfying to those who read it. Our obligation would seem to vary with the portion of the story and we have to focus on different considerations depending on whether we're dealing with the beginning, the middle, or the end.

To depart from our nautical metaphor, the beginning of a story is a snare. We have to engage the reader's attention. We have to draw him in and trap him, and the more effective our trap, the more likely we will have him for the duration.

The middle of the story is a joyride. We don't have to be so competitive now because there's less competition out there. With every paragraph, the reader considers himself to have a greater investment in what he's reading. It's easy for him to quit on the first or second page, much harder to jump overboard and start swimming when we've had him with us for half a dozen pages of a story or as many chapters of a novel.

The ending of the story is the payoff. It's the promised destination that draws him onto your boat in the first place. (The nautical motif seems inescapable, doesn't it? I can't manage to shake it.) If the ending doesn't deliver, the reader feels cheated by the entire experience. He may have enjoyed himself all along, but he's apt to forget that now; all he'll recall later is that he finished with a feeling of considerable dissatisfaction. "The first chapter sells the book," Mickey Spillane has said of his own work. "The last chapter sells the *next* book."

Let's talk about beginnings.

PIPING THEM ABOARD

The first chapter sells the book. The first page sells the story.

And it is there at the beginning that good salesmanship is most important.

In the introduction to one of his books of poetry, e.e. cummings explained that his poems were in competition, not only with other poems but with flowers and balloons and mud puddles and train rides and, indeed, with everything that might occupy a prospective reader's attention. Our fiction is similarly competitive and it is essential for me to remember that nobody has to read something simply because I had to write it. A couple of people—my agent, my editor—have to go through the motions, but their eyes glaze over, they turn pages without paying too much attention to the words contained thereon. Nobody else has to turn the pages. No one has to print what I've written; once it has been printed, no one is obliged to buy it; the person who buys it can stop reading after a paragraph and pick up something else instead, or watch television, or go out and mow the lawn.

It is my job to keep this from happening, and I can best assure this by starting out right.

Sometime last year I picked up *A Study in Scarlet*, Sir Arthur Conan Doyle's classic novel of Sherlock Holmes. I blush to admit that I had never read it before. (I do a lot of this sort of blushing. The list of acknowledged literary masterpieces that I have unaccountably missed is a lengthy one. The books could fill a library—and, come to think of it, often do.)

The first thing that struck me about *A Study in Scarlet* was that it could never have been published today in the form in which it appears. The book takes forever to get underway. Watson talks about he met Holmes, describes their lodgings, and provides a wealth of admittedly absorbing detail before anything happens. That a novel should take so much time getting started seems incomprehensible to us a century later, and it becomes even more remarkable when we recall that *A Study in Scarlet* first appeared as a magazine serial. I don't know just where the first installment ended, but it's unlikely that it could have contained more than a bare hint of the story itself.

Would a contemporary editor reject Conan Doyle's novel? Not necessarily. The writing is so good and the characterization so engaging that a good editor might well stay with the book through its desultory opening, and then get wholly caught up in the book's narrative flow. But that same editor would certainly insist that the author refashion the opening in order to make the story more accessible to the reader.

Ought the book to be revised today to accommodate the tastes of modern readers? No, certainly not. *A Study in Scarlet* has been in print since its first appearance, and it seems likely to remain in print as long as people read books in English—or in any of the dozens of other languages into which it has been translated. It does just fine in its present form, and it would be a travesty to alter a word.

But today's reader knows what he is getting when he picks the book up. He knows, for openers, that the book is a classic, that it has delighted generations of readers, and that he can be certain of a rousing tale and a fascinating cast of characters. He knows who Holmes and Watson are, and knows that at least half of the pleasure of the book will be the delight of their company during its reading. He is, in short, presold. The book could open any damn way and he's going to stay with it.

You and I are not in that enviable position. (Neither, when the book first appeared, was Conan Doyle, but he lived in different times. Readers were less hurried, and they very likely had fewer alternate pastimes available to them. Even so, he would not have been ill-advised to get the game afoot a little closer to page one.)

In a couple of columns over the years I've written about opening paragraphs and their function in getting things off to a good start. But the beginning of the story or novel amounts to more than a couple of paragraphs. It is, indeed, as much as it takes to pipe your reader abroad, to get him hooked even as you get the story going.

You have to manage several things at once. First, of course, you have to attract his attention and draw him in. You may try to accomplish this by beginning with the action already in progress; later on, you and he will both have time to take a breath and put your feet up, and you can fill him in on the whys and wherefores of what he's been watching.

This is a handy device, but it's not the only way to start quickly. You can open with a provocative statement about the story or one of its characters. ("Most people take a lifetime to learn life's most important lesson. Jack Bayliss learned everything he had to know in five minutes one September afternoon on the leeward side of a West Virginia mountain.") You can use a background anecdote. ("When Audrey was a baby she was always a picky eater. Years afterward, her mother would tell anyone who listened about the day she tried to get the child to eat an artichoke. . . .")

At the same time that you engage the reader's attention, you want to let him know what kind of a story he's reading. This task is not a burden to be carried exclusively by the beginning of the text. The title will share the load, along with the blurbs, the jacket copy, the cover art, the promotional campaign, and whatever reputation your previous work has earned you. All of these elements have combined to give the reader an idea of what to expect from your book, but he will still not entirely have made up his mind when he reads your opening, and it can either increase his appetite for what follows or put him off altogether.

Some years ago a friend strongly urged me to read *Another Roadside Attraction*, Tom Robbins's brilliant first novel. I dutifully picked up the book in a store, read the first two pages, and put it back. A few weeks later my friend asked if I'd read the book.

"I started to," I said, "but I could tell it wasn't my kind of thing."

"It is absolutely and unequivocally your kind of thing," he said. "I'll bet you got bogged down in the first two pages, didn't you? I should have warned you about that. Pick it up again and bull your way past the first two pages, or skip them if you have to. They're false advertising, because the book's completely different from what they'd lead you to expect."

A further chore of the beginning is to make you care about the story, to convince you that you ought to give a damn how it turns out. In a recent column I mentioned how I'd have a slight problem in this regard with my novel, *Out on the Cutting Edge*. While the beginning was smooth enough, and while there was enough movement to keep the reader from dozing off, the book seemed to my editor to lack a sense of urgency. She felt the reader would wonder why my detective hero, Matthew Scudder, would care all that much about the fate and whereabouts of a young woman he's hired to find. We've never seen the woman, and neither has he, and we're thus not all that concerned about her, and wonder why he would be.

I solved this problem by adding a prologue in which Scudder imagines the woman's last day. The chapters that follow are unchanged; we still don't see her, and neither does Scudder, but we've had a strong hint that something terrible will turn out to have happened to her, and we've established that there's some kind of psychic bond between her and the detective. We believe that he feels as though he knows her, and we even feel as though we've met her—but of course we haven't.

KEEPING THEM ON THE SHIP

For a great many writers, the middle of a story presents the greatest problem. This is less noticeably the case with short fiction, where there's simply less ground to be covered between the start and the finish. (The shortest of stories may be said to have no middle; the beginning leads almost directly to the ending.) In the novel, however, most of the book is middle. A chapter or two gets the book underway, and a chapter or two later on will finish it off, but between the two stretches an endless tunnel, a bottomless abyss, a vastness beyond measure. Page after page of innocent paper has to be filled with words, all of them well-chosen and placed in some presumably agreeable order.

The most self-assured of writers is apt to suffer a crisis of confidence during a book's lengthy midsection. His nightmare tends to be twofold. First, there's the mounting concern that the book will never be done, that the middle will extend forever, that each new page he writes will bring him farther from the beginning but not a whit closer to the end.

(There is, incidentally, an alternative to this concern. The writer becomes anxious that the middle will be too short, that he cannot possibly pad it out long enough to fulfill either the general requirements of the fiction market or the specific ones of his own contract. I have on occasion had both of these worries at the same time, and have sat at the typewriter simultaneously alarmed that my book was going to be too long and that it would wind up too short. It is, let me assure you, a curious matter to write scene after scene not knowing whether you should be padding them or cutting them short. If you induce a comparable neurotic state in a lab rat, he sits down in the middle of the maze and chews off his own feet.)

Besides worrying over the long and short of it, the writer is typically concerned that what he's shouting is going to fall on deaf ears, or on no ears at all. The reader, cunningly hooked by the book's beginning, will dislodge that hook and swim off into the sunset.

And, indeed, this happens. I don't finish every book I start reading, and I somehow doubt I'm unique in this regard. While I once felt some sort of moral obligation to wade through every book I picked up, somewhere around age 35 I outgrew this foolishness. In this world, one of many books and little time, I feel comfortable occasionally leaving another writer's book unfinished.

But the thought that someone—anyone!—would abandon one of *my* books . . . well, that's another matter entirely.

Some of my concern in this regard may derive from my own literary apprenticeship. I started off writing soft-core sex novels, and the experience left me imprinted with the notion that, if I ever let a whole chapter go by without someone either making love or getting killed, I was waving a beige flag at the reader's attention span.

While this left me with some bad habits that I had to learn to break, I think I was probably luckier than some writers who emerge from an academic background and start off writing thoughtful, introspective novels in which there is not a great deal of dramatic incident. All things considered, I would rather give too much than too little attention to holding the reader's interest.

THE RIDE OF THEIR LIVES

How do you keep the reader aboard? How do you keep him reading?

The first thing to remember is that he *wants* to keep on reading. He picked up the book in the hope that it would engross him utterly. The most compelling blurbs in ads and on book jackets are those which assure you that the book, once begun, cannot possibly be set aside. I know any number of people who read books in order to get to sleep at night, yet no one would try to sell a book by hailing its soporific properties. "This book kept me up all night" is a far more effective promotional claim than "This book lulled me right into a coma."

More than he wants insight or laughter or tears, and far more than he wants his life changed, the reader wants something that will keep him reading. Once hooked by your opening, he has an investment of time along with his investment of money in your book. Every additional page he reads increases his investment and commits him more deeply to finish what he has started.

So you have a lot going for you. The reader would prefer to stay with you, to see the book through to the end, to have a good time on the way.

All you have to do is keep him amused.

And how do you do that? Here a few ways:

Have Interesting Things Happen

Most of the books I've written in recent years have been detective stories. While the category is broad enough to embrace a wide range of novels, a common denominator exists in that a lead character is almost invariably called upon to do a certain amount of detecting. This very often involves going around and talking to people.

When my detective hero, Matthew Scudder, goes around knocking on doors and asking questions, he's acquiring information that serves to advance the plot. But if these scenes did no more than provide him with data, they would make very tedious reading indeed. It is not enough that they be functional in terms of the book's plot. It is also essential that they be interesting.

In *Eight Million Ways to Die*, for example, Scudder is hired by a pimp to investigate the murder of one of the pimp's girls. He pursues the investigation by interviewing each of his client's surviving girls. Writing these scenes, I took pains to make each interesting in and of itself. I did this by letting the women emerge as individuals, with their own separate histories, personalities and current lifestyles. Their different perceptions of the pimp enlarged the reader's understanding of that enigmatic character, too.

Every scene you write can be more or less interesting depending on how you write it. Not every scene deserves full treatment, and there will be times when you'll hurry things along by summarizing a scene in a couple of sentences. But the more space you give to a scene and the more importance you assign to it, the greater is your obligation to make that scene pull its weight by commanding the reader's attention and keeping him interested and entertained.

Keep the Story Moving

The reader will accept a lot of diversionary scenes, if they're diverting enough. But you don't want to do such a good job on this that he forgets the point of the whole thing.

In the broadest sense, fiction is about the solution

(successful or not) of a problem. If the reader loses sight of that problem during the book's vast middle, he ceases to care. He may keep reading out of inertia if you provide enough entertainment along the way, but if anything comes along to break his attention, he may not get around to picking up the book again. Even if he does keep reading, you may lose your hold on his emotions.

Several times in recent books I've stopped along the way to rewrite a chapter, cutting scenes down or chopping them out entirely. They were entertaining enough as written, and I had to chop out and throw away some nice snappy dialogue that I felt rather proud of—because it was slowing the book's narrative flow. I feel the need to do this as I go along because I'm not comfortable otherwise, but many writers find it works better if they let their scenes run on and do their cutting after the first draft is finished. In either case, the same considerations operate.

Pile on the Miseries

One thing you want to do in the book's middle is turn up the gain on your narrative. You do this by making the problem more of a headache. This makes its solution more essential.

In suspense fiction, a standard way to do this is to toss another corpse on the floor. The reader is already committed to the idea that the initial murder must be solved and the murderer apprehended. When someone else dies, such a resolution becomes even more imperative. Furthermore, you've introduced an element of urgency; the hero must act not only to restore balance to the universe, but also to prevent the death of other characters, including some who may by now have become important to the reader.

Similarly, you can raise the stakes for the reader by making the problem harder to solve. In *A Ticket to the Boneyard*, a just-completed novel about Scudder, he is trying to apprehend a particularly vicious killer. While he is struggling to track the man down, several things happen to heighten the tension and raise the stakes. There are additional murders. Scudder gets severely beaten. And his closest friend on the police force turns on him, denying him support he'd come to take for granted.

Enjoy the Trip

Some people enjoy writing. Others hate it. As far as I can tell, there's no real correlation between the pleasure the author takes in a book's composition and the pleasure a reader will take later.

Even so, I suspect we're well advised to have as much fun with all of this as we possibly can. And it's the middle of the book that is most apt to appear burdensome when we're bogged down in it. If writing a book is driving across America, the book's middle is an endless highway across Kansas, and there are days when every sentence is as flat as the unvarying landscape.

There are, to be sure, a lot of interesting things in Kansas. But you won't enjoy them much if you spend every moment telling yourself you can't wait to get to California, and if you're twitching with anxiety that book will be too long or too short or just plain lousy.

Forget all that. Stay in the now. Enjoy the trip.

A while back a friend of mine was flying from Los Angeles to New York. He was in the first-class section, a luxury to which he is not much accustomed, and the chap seated beside him was some sort of yuppie businessman, on his way to or from some sort of hostile takeover. The little swine had a clear enough conscience to lose himself altogether in the inflight movie, a pleasure my friend was willing to forgo.

The yuppie laughed immoderately all through the film. When he unplugged his earphones even as they rolled the final credits, my friend asked him how he'd liked it.

"Not so great," the young man said.

"But you laughed your head off," my friend protested. "If you hadn't been belted in you'd have fallen out of your seat."

"Oh, I'm not saying it wasn't funny," the little shark replied. "There were some great laughs in the thing. But, you know, it just wasn't a very good picture."

Now this story might do little more than illustrate the perversity of the Young Undeservedly Prosperous but for the specific film involved. It was *Burglar*, the Whoopi Goldberg vehicle based (more or less) on a book called *The Burglar in the Closet*, a mystery novel written by, uh, me. And the chap seated beside the chortling little chiseler was my agent, the redoubtable Knox Burger.

And, worst of all, the damned whelp was right. *Burglar* was a million laughs, but it just wasn't a very good movie. And virtually everyone who saw it reacted pretty much the way Knox's seatmate did. They roared while they were in the theater, and then they told their friends not to bother going. This was true of the insider audiences; laughter was riotous at the large Manhattan house where I saw the film screened, and the very people who laughed the loudest then went home and wrote scathingly negative reviews. The reaction was the same at the theaters in suburban shopping malls. Everybody had a good time for ninety minutes and went out shaking the old head in disgust.

Why should a film—or fiction in any form—provoke this sort of contradictory response? How could audiences have such a good time with the picture while it was going on and respect it so little once it was over? In the particular case of *Burglar*, I think there are several answers. The gags were too easy, the characterizations were shallow, the relationships were too hard-edged—there were lots of things wrong with this movie, and most of them need not concern us here. But one factor that I'm sure contributed to the film's failure to generate good word-of-mouth was the relative weakness of its ending. The ending was soft, and it left the audience unsatisfied.

"The first chapter sells the book," Mickey Spillane has said. "The last chapter sells the *next* book."

Very true. But there's even more to it than that. The last chapter sells the next book by convincing the reader that the book he's just finished was terrific. That doesn't just make him a customer for your next effort, but it makes him a powerful salesman for what he's just finished reading. The stronger your ending, the more likely he'll be to recommend the book to his friends. It is word-of-mouth that ultimately creates bestsellers. Nothing else, no amount of advertising and publicity, can sustain a book that does not get touted by those who read it. And a book with an unsatisfying ending just cannot generate strong world-of-mouth on a broad scale.

THE END?

If, as we're always being told, a work of fiction has a beginning, a middle, and an ending, it seems reasonable to suppose that a writer is variously challenged by each of these three components. His job in the beginning is to hook the reader into the story, while in the middle it is his task simply to keep the person reading.

At the end, he has to pay off all the book's promises. He has to give the reader everything he signed on for—and more. A weak ending can kill a good book, and a really powerful ending can save a book with not that much else going for it.

During the past year I've read a pair of unusually well-written first novels, both of them suspense yarns, one set in Michigan, the other in the Florida Keys. Both books have generated a lot of favorable comment among mystery pros, no doubt because of the genuine excellence of their writing. Neither did as well with the public at large, and I think I know why. The ending of one was improbable, almost silly, while the other ended very inconclusively. I enjoyed both immensely while I was reading them, but ended feeling somehow cheated and unsatisfied.

I know I've hurt my own sales in the same fashion in at least one book. *Ariel*, a novel I published many years ago, was a story of a psychological suspense featuring a twelve-year-old girl who may or may not be evil, and who may or may not have murdered her baby brother in his crib. And the ending is inconclusive. You don't find out for sure what the girl is and what she did. A few reviewers liked the enigmatic ending, but more than a few did not, and I don't blame them. It was vague because I was vague—I didn't know what had happened. I would have greatly preferred a less uncertain ending if I could only have come up with one.

BUT WOULD IT MAKE IT ON MTV?

What makes an ending work?

Maybe the best way to answer that is to listen to a Beethoven symphony. By the time the last note of the coda has sounded at the end of the fourth movement, you damn well know it's over. When the last ringing chord hits you, every musical question has been answered, every emotional issue has been resolved, and you don't have to wait for the folks around you to start applauding in order to be certain the piece is done. If Ludwig van B. had set *Ariel* to music, there wouldn't have been anything enigmatic about the ending, believe me.

SETTING SIGHTS

It's generally a good deal easier to write an ending with impact if you have that ending in mind from the onset. The more clearly you are able to perceive it as you go along, the more you can shape the various elements of the story so that the ending will resolve them in a satisfying fashion.

Does this mean that you have to have the whole book outlined, in your mind or on paper, before you write it? As one who almost never uses an outline, I'm hardly inclined to advance such an argument. It is possible, however, to know your ending without knowing just how you're going to reach it.

Several novelists, most recently E.L. Doctorow, have likened the writing of a novel to driving at night. You can see only as far as your headlight beams reach, but you can drive clear across country that way.

Very true, and I've written any number of books in just that fashion. But I've been most successful when, while I could not see past the range of my headlights, I nevertheless knew my ultimate destination in advance. If I just hop in the car with no goal in mind, I may have an enjoyable journey, but I run the risk of not getting anywhere, or not even really knowing when the trip is over. (In point of fact I travel that way all the time in real life, but it doesn't work as well in fiction.)

Dorothy Salisbury Davis, who does very well indeed with beginnings and middles as well as endings, has said that she can't comfortably write a mystery novel unless she knows from the onset who did it. She may change her mind in the course of the book, she may wind up hanging the murder on someone other than her initial choice, but she always has a solution in mind even as she constructs the problem.

I haven't always done this, but I certainly have an easier time when I do. It seems to me, too, that a substantial portion of the books I've abandoned over the years have been ones for which I did not have a strong ending in mind from the beginning. I ran out of gas on those books not specifically because I wound up painting myself into a corner or wandering in an insoluble maze but simply because each book sort of wobbled to a halt. I think it may have been a lack of a concrete destination in the form of a foreseen ending that brought this about.

FINAL LEG OF THE JOURNEY

The most satisfactory endings resolve everything. Like that Beethoven coda we just heard, they answer questions we never even thought to ask.

Most of my books are mystery novels, concerned with a crime and its solution. Find the murderer and you've found the ending. Mysteries, however, are frequently concerned with more than crime and punishment, and sometimes an ending has to do more than name a perpetrator and clap the cuffs on him.

Eight Million Ways to Die is a good case in point. The book begins with the murder of a call girl, and my detective, Matthew Scudder, is hired by her pimp to find out who killed her. The stakes are raised when two other prostitutes die, one an apparent suicide. And, finally, Scudder brings the killer to justice. He does so by making himself a stalking horse, a move that almost fails when the killer waits in Scudder's hotel room with a machete. But Scudder and justice prevail, and the bad guy gets what's coming to him, and the ending is dramatically satisfying.

But the string of murders is not all that the book is about. It's also about life and death in New York, and it's very much about Scudder's attempt to come to terms with his alcoholism. He struggles to stay sober as he chases the killer through the city's terrible streets, and the book follows him in and out of gin mills and detox wards and AA meetings. After the book has seemingly ended, after the killer has been found out and dealt with and the solution explained to his client, there is a final chapter in which Scudder is brought face to face with his own illness and has to confront himself or back down.

The first ending—the unmasking and apprehension of the killer—is dramatically effective but not everything it might be. Because of the story itself, the killer is not someone we have met before. (Hollywood can't bear this sort of thing, and in the film version the killer is the sneering villain we've met early on.) But the second ending more than makes up for it. A considerable number of people have told me, in person or through the mails, how much impact the ending had for them. Many of them have assured me that they cried, that they were moved to tears.

And that is what an ending ought to do. It ought to move a reader. It need not move him to tears—although that doesn't hurt. But it ought to leave him knowing that he's been in a fight and that the fight is over. You don't have to leave him feeling happy—although a downbeat ending is usually hard to bring off effectively. But you do have to leave him feeling complete. He may finish wondering what will happen to the characters afterward, and that's all right as long as you leave him feeling that the issues raised in this part of their story are resolved.

Not every successful book has an ending that works in this sense. Some people break the rules and seem to get away with it. The example that comes first to mind for me is John le Carré, who has made an occasional habit of endings that I can only assume are intentionally obscure. Both *The Spy Who Came in From the Cold* and *A Small Town in Germany* have ambiguous last pages; you have to read them over a second or third time in order to be certain just what is taking place. The author's writing is so clear elsewhere that it is puzzling that his ending should be so murky. I can't seriously argue that this weakness, if that's what it is, has hurt le Carré with readers or critics. He's doing just fine, and for all I know maybe I'm the only person who finds his endings opaque.

Any questions? Yes, Rachel?

Why "kill them at the end," sir? Why such a violent image?

I don't know, Rachel. I've asked myself the same question, and originally looked around for a way to paraphrase Donald Westlake's original observation that triggered this series of observations. But I can't find an alternative that works as well.

Comedians, and performers in general, use that metaphor. "I killed them in Keokuk," the vaudevillian would say. "I knocked them dead. I beat their brains in. I slaughtered them."

I guess the implication is that the audience—and in our case the reader—is overpowered by the material. It overwhelms him, and killing is the ultimate way of being overwhelmed because it is undeniably final. What you may be objecting to, Rachel, is the implication of hostility between the comic and his audience, the writer and his reader. If you're trying to kill your readers, doesn't that mean that you hate them?

No, not in this case, not when they pick up the book hoping to be killed in just this fashion. Even if you continue to dislike the metaphor, I'd urge you to strive for fictional endings that seem to fit it. Because this kind of metaphoric death is anything but final. Unless you kill them at the end, they won't keep coming back for more.

The Use of the Journal in Writing a Private Eye Novel

Sue Grafton

The most valuable tool I employ in the writing of a private eye novel is the working journal. The process is one I began in rudimentary form when I first started work on *"A" Is for Alibi*, though all I retain of that journal now are a few fragmentary notes. With *"B" Is for Burglar*, I began to refine the method and from *"C" Is for Corpse* on, I've kept a daily log of work in progress. This notebook (usually four times longer than the novel itself) is like a letter to myself, detailing every idea that occurs to me as I proceed. Some ideas I incorporate, some I modify, many I discard. The journal is a record of my imagination at work, from the first spark of inspiration to the final manuscript. Here I record my worries and concerns, my dead ends, my occasional triumphs, all the difficulties I face as the narrative unfolds. The journal contains solutions to all the problems that arise in the course of the writing. Sometimes the breakthroughs are sudden; more often the answers are painstakingly arrived at through trial and error.

One of my theories about writing is that the process involves an ongoing interchange between Left Brain and Right. The journal provides a testing ground where the two can engage. Left Brain is analytical, linear, the time keeper, the bean counter, the critic and editor, a valuable ally in the shaping of the mystery novel or any piece of writing for that matter. Right Brain is creative, spatial, playful, disorganized, dazzling, nonlinear, the source of the *Aha!* or imaginative leap. Without Right Brain, there would be no material for Left Brain to refine. Without Left Brain, the jumbled brilliance of Right Brain would never coalesce into a satisfactory whole.

In addition to the yin/yang of the bicameral brain, the process of writing is a constant struggle between the Ego and the Shadow, to borrow Jungian terms. Ego, as implied, is the public aspect of our personality, the carefully constructed personna, or mask, we present to the world as the "truth" about us. The Shadow is our Unconscious, the Dark Side—the dangerous, largely unacknowledged cauldron of "unacceptable" feelings and reactions that we'd prefer not to look at in ourselves and certainly hope to keep hidden from others. We spend the bulk of our lives perfecting our public image, trying to deny or eradicate the perceived evil in our nature.

For the writer, however—especially the mystery writer— the Shadow is crucial. The Shadow gives us access to our repressed rage, the murderous impulses that propel antisocial behavior whether we're inclined to act out or not. Without ingress to our own Shadow, we would have no way to delineate the nature of a fictional killer, no way to penetrate and depict the inner life of the villain in the novels we write. As mystery writers, we probe this emotional black swamp again and again, dredging in the muck for plot and character. As repelled as we may be by the Dark Side of our nature, we're drawn to its power, recognizing that the Shadow contains enormous energy if we can tap into it. The journal is the writer's invitation to the Shadow, a means of beckoning to the Unconscious, enticing it to yield its potent magic to the creative process.

WHAT GOES INTO THE JOURNAL AND HOW DOES IT WORK?

At the outset of each new novel, the first thing I do is open a document on my word processor that I call "Notes" or

"Notes-1." By the end of a book, I have four or five such documents, averaging fifty single-spaced pages apiece.

In my first act of the writing day, I log into my journal with the date. Usually I begin with a line about what's happening in my life. I make a note if I'm coming down with a cold, if my cat's run away, if I've got company coming in from out of town. Anything that specifically characterizes the day becomes part of the journal on the theory that exterior events have the potential to affect the day's work. If I have a bad day at work, I can sometimes track the problem to its source and try correcting it there. For instance, if I'm consistently distracted every time I'm scheduled for a speaking engagement, I can limit outside events until the book is done.

The second entry in the journal is a note about any idea that's occurred to me in the dead of night, when Shadow and Right Brain are most active. Often, I'm wakened by a nudge from Right Brain with some suggestion about where to go next in the narrative or offering a reminder of a beat I've missed. Sometimes, I'm awakened by emotion-filled dreams or the horror of a nightmare, either one of which can hold clues about the story I'm working on. It's my contention that our writing is a window to all of our internal attitudes and emotional states. If I sit down to write and I'm secretly worried about the progress I'm making, then that worry will infuse the very work itself. If I'm anxious about an upcoming scene, if I'm troubled by the pacing, if I suspect a plot is too convoluted, or the identity of the killer is too transparent, then the same anxiety will inhibit the flow of words. Until I own my worries, I run the risk of self-sabotage or writer's block. The journal serves as a place to off-load anxiety, a verbal repair shop when my internal writing machine breaks down.

Generally, the next step in the journal is to lay out for myself where I am in the book. I talk to myself about the scene I'm working on, or the trouble spots as I see them. It's important to realize that the journal in progress is absolutely private—*for my eyes only*. This is not a literary *oeuvre* in which I preen and posture for some future biographer. This is a nuts-and-bolts format in which I think aloud, fret, whine and wring my hands. There's nothing grand about it and it's certainly not meant to be great writing. Once a novel is finished and out on the shelves, then the journal can be opened to public inspection if I so choose.

In the safety of the journal, I can play "Suppose . . ." and "What if . . ." creating an atmosphere of open debate where Ego and Shadow, Left Brain and Right, can all be heard. I write down all the story possibilities . . . all the pros and cons . . . and then check back a day or so later to see which prospects strike a chord. The journal is experimental. The journal functions as a playground for the mind, a haven where the imagination can cavort at will. While I'm working in the journal, I don't have to look good. I can be as dumb or goofy as I want. The journal provides a place where I can let my proverbial hair down and "dare to be stupid," as we used to say in Hollywood.

The beauty of the journal entry is that before I know it, I'm sliding right into my writing for the day. Instead of feeling resistant or hesitant, the journal provides a jump-start, a way to get the words moving.

To demonstrate the technique, I'll include a few sample pages from the journal I kept during the writing of *"G" Is for Gumshoe*. I do this without embarrassment (she said), though I warn you in advance that what you see is a fumbling process, my tortured mind at work.

"G" Is for Gumshoe is essentially a "road picture." In this seventh novel in the series, Kinsey Millhone discovers she's on Tyrone Patty's hit list, targeted for assassination in retaliation for her part in his arrest and conviction. The following passages of the journal begin some three chapters into the novel. Earlier notes, unfortunately, were lost to me in the transfer of the work from an old computer system to newly acquired equipment. My intention here is not to try to dazzle you with my song-and-dance work, but to demonstrate the mundane level at which the journal actually functions.

1-2-89

Just checking in to have a little chat. I'm in Chapter 3 and feeling pretty good, but I'm wondering if I don't need some tension or suspense. We know there may be a hit man after her. She's currently on her way to the desert and everything seems really normal . . . nay, even dull. Do I need to pep it up a bit? She's almost at the Slabs. I've been doing a lot of description but maybe I need to weave it into the narrative better. Flipping back and forth from the external to the internal.

What other possibilities are there? I've noticed that with Dick Francis, sometimes when nothing's happening, you sit there expecting something anyway. I could use the external as a metaphor for the internal. I know I'll be doing that when Dietz enters the scene. What could Kinsey be thinking about while she drives down to the Slabs? She's talked briefly . . .

1-4-89

Can't remember what I meant to say in the paragraph above. I did some work last night that I'm really happy with. I'm using a little boy with a toy car at the rest stop. Added a father asleep on the bench. Later, he turns out to be one of the guys hired to kill her.

Want to remember to use a couple of things.

1. When the mother dies, Kinsey goes back down to the desert with Dietz. They search, finding nothing . . . maybe a few personal papers. What they come across, in an old cardboard box under the trailer, is some objects . . . maybe just old cups & saucers (which may trigger memories in Irene Gersh . . .). But the newspapers in which these objects are packed dated back to 1937 . . . Santa Teresa. Obviously, the mother was there at some point.

When Kinsey checks into the mother's background, she realizes Irene's birth certificate is a total fake. The mother has whited out the real information, typed over it, and has done a photocopy. All the information has been falsified. She's not who she says she was during her lifetime . . . father's name is wrong . . . I was thinking it might be Santa Teresa, but then Irene would know at the outset she had some connection with the town. Better she should think she was born in Brawley or someplace like that.

Kinsey tries to track down the original in San Diego . . . or wherever I decide to place the original . . . no record of such a birth. Once Kinsey finds the old newspapers, she decides to try Santa Teresa records, using the certificate # which is the only thing that hasn't been tampered with. Up comes the true certificate.

Must remember that a social security card . . . first three digits indicate where the card was issued. That might be a clue.

Irene Gersh is floored. If mom isn't who she claims she was, then who am I?

Must also remember that mom is frightened to death. That would be a nice murder method.

In addition to storyboarding ideas, I use my journal to record notes for all the research I've done. I also make a note of any question that occurs to me while I'm writing a scene. Instead of stopping the flow of words, I simply jot down a memo to myself for later action.

Journals often contain the ideas for scenes, characters, plot twists or clever lines of dialogue that don't actually make it into the book I'm working on. Such literary detritus might well provide the spark for the next book in the series.

Often, too, in the pages of a journal, I'll find Right Brain leaping ahead to a later scene in the book. Since I don't actually outline a novel in any format or detailed way, the journal is a road map to the story I'm working on. If dialogue or a descriptive passage suddenly occurs to me, I'll tuck it in the journal and come back to it when I reach the chapter where the excerpt belongs. This way, I find I can do some of my writing in advance of myself. Right Brain, my creative part, really isn't interested in working line-by-line. Right Brain sees the whole picture, like the illustration on the box that contains a jigsaw puzzle. Left Brain might insist that we start at the beginning and proceed in an orderly fashion right through to the end, but Right Brain has its own way of going about its business. The journal is a place to honor Right Brain's ingenuity and nonconformity.

Sometimes I use the journal to write a note directly to Shadow or Right Brain, usually when I'm feeling blocked or stuck. These notes are like writer's prayers and I'm always astonished at how quickly they're answered.

In the *"G" Is for Gumshoe* journal, you can see that by March, some three months later, the book has advanced almost magically. I'll do a hop-skip-and-jump, picking up entries here and there.

3-12-89

Finally got Dietz & Kinsey on the road. They've stopped for lunch. She's asking him about his background & he's being good about that stuff. Want to keep them moving . . . let information surface while they're heading for Santa Teresa. Don't want the story to come to a screeching halt while they chit chat. Must keep defining his character through action . . . not just dialogue. Once I get the book on body-guarding techniques, I can fill in some technical information that will make him seem very knowledgeable. For now, I can do the small touches. At some point, he should give her some rules & regulations.

What else do I want to accomplish on the way up to Santa Teresa? Don't need any action at this point . . . don't need jeopardy per se. Must keep in mind that Dick Francis plays relationships very nicely without jamming incessant screams and chases into the narrative.

3-13-89

I wonder if chapter nine will last all the way to Santa
Teresa. What does Kinsey do when she gets home? She'll
call Irene to make sure Agnes has arrived, which she will
very soon. She'll introduce Dietz to Henry Pitts who'll be
briefed about the situation re: the hit man. Security mea-
sures (if I knew what they were . . .)

Want to dovetail "A" & "B" plots so both won't come to
a ragged stop simultaneously.

Within a day, Agnes Grey will have disappeared from
the nursing home.

Soon after, her body will be found.

Haven't quite solved the problem of how Kinsey gets
hired to track down the killer.

Can't quite decide what the next beat is in the attempt
on Kinsey's life. Dietz will get her a bullet proof vest. Does
he jog with her? She won't really feel like it and he'll advise
against. He'll have her take a different route to the office
& home every day . . . always in his company.

Maybe Dietz has to make a quick trip to Carson City . . . or
someplace. Papa sick? Mama sick? An unavoidable personal
emergency. If I played my cards right, his absence might
coincide with Kinsey's second trip to the desert. I guess
I'll map all this out as I get to it but it does feel like a tricky
business to make the story move smoothly through here.

Why do I worry so much about boring the reader? I don't
want it to look like I've sacrificed the mystery and the pace
for mere romance.

And skipping ahead to August . . .

8-12-89

Trying not to panic here. In the dead of night, Right
Brain suggested that maybe Kinsey gets locked in the very
storage bin Agnes was locked in. Nice claustrophobic

atmosphere.

As a reader, I don't object to being privy to the reasoning process a detective goes through as long as it makes sense to me and seems logical. When the leap comes too fast, then I object. I like for the detective to consider every possible alternative.

My problem here is one of transitions . . . forging the links between the scenes I know are coming up.

8-15-89

Book was due today but so be it. Just closed out Chapter 23 and opened 24. I'm going to write notes to myself for a while and then print pages 30-35 so I can have them handy.

Need to set up "It used to be Sumner . . ."

Maybe Kinsey & Dietz go back to Irene's & confront her with the true information on the birth certificate. If these aren't my parents, then who am I?

8-16-89

God, I'm tired today. I'd really love to sleep. Let's see what I can accomplish in a stupor. Can't wait for this book to be over and done.

Dear Right Brain,

Please be with me here and help me solve and resolve the remaining questions in the narrative. Help me to be resourceful, imaginative, energetic, inventive. And patient.

Look forward to hearing from you.

Sincerely,

Sue

I could pull up countless other samples, but you get the point I'm sure.

One comfort I take from my journals is that regardless of where I am in the current private eye novel, I can always peek back into the journals I've kept for previous books and discover that I was just as confused and befuddled back *then* as I am today. Prior journals are reminders that regardless of past struggles, I did somehow manage to prevail. Having survived through two novels, or five, or even twelve, in my case, there's some reason to suppose that I'll survive to write the next.

If you haven't already incorporated a journal or its equivalent into your current bag of writing tricks, you might try your hand at one and see how it works for you. Remember, it's your journal and you can do it any way you choose. If you don't use a PC, you can write yours in crayon on 10 × 14 sheets of newsprint. You can type it, write in longhand, use a code if you need to feel protected. You can log in every day or only once a week. You can use it as a launching pad and then abandon the practice, or use it as I do, as an emotional tether connecting me to each day's work.

To help you get started, I'll give you the first entry just to speed you on your way:

Enter today's date.

Just sitting down here to try my hand at this weird stuff Sue Grafton has been talking about. A lot of it sounds like California psychobabble, but if it helps with the writing, who really cares?

In the book I'm working on what worried me is . . .

And the Murderer Is . . .

Loren D. Estleman

kay, so the missing heiress is locked in a soundproof cell on the top floor of the abandoned sanitarium, the stolen sapphires are in a black velvet pouch on the examining table in the old shock-therapy room, and a bookend set of hired thugs is holding your detective at bay with big automatics while a disembodied voice boasts over the intercom of having committed every successful crime since the sinking of the *U.S.S. Maine.*

Whose voice is it? And how do you fuse together all the loose fragments you've been scattering willy-nilly throughout the previous three hundred pages without making your climactic scene read like the autobiography of a former mayor of Cleveland?

The overwhelming majority of PI stories that go wrong do so at the point where the solution is revealed. This is fatal, as it is precisely for this scene that the long-suffering reader has kept dozens of seamy neon-lit liaisons, sat through pages of tight-jawed dialogue, gnawed his nails through a couple of car chases, and withstood untold numbers of brutal beatings. Once there, flushed and breathless, he finds himself being *talked to* by the suddenly long-winded detective—or worse, the murderer. His eyes glaze. His attention wanders. He counts the number of pages remaining. Oh, he goes ahead and finishes; at twenty bucks and up for the average hardcover novel and three-fifty at rock bottom for paperback—not counting his time investment so far—he's not about to give it up at this late date. But he won't buy another book by the same author. Bored he can get in front of the tube for free.

Chances are the book won't get even that far. Multiply that investment by a thousand, and any editorial board worthy of the name will likely pass in favor of a slim volume by the latest avant-garde poet to appear at a presidential inauguration.

AVOID SOLILOQUIES

Suspension of disbelief is a high-wire act, requiring enough plausibility on one end of the balance pole to counter the pull of audacious invention on the other. While the reader will for the sake of a good story and a challenging mystery accept the fact that your detective behaves in a fashion more worthy of St. George than the workaday professional investigator of the real world, he will question why that same St. George is allowed to hold forth at jaw-breaking length on timetables, motives and minute clues without someone interrupting him. Soliloquies served Shakespeare well, but in a world plunging chin-first toward the twenty-first century, no one, actual or created, has either the time or the patience to sit still for speeches outside the confines of the Friars Club.

Nor will the writer avoid this sand trap by assigning exposition to a character other than his detective. One of my personal bugbears is the boastful villain. We're all familiar with this turkey: the criminal mastermind who gets the drop on the hero, then says something like, "I'm going to kill you, but before I do, let me tell you why I did what I did and how I did it." In view of the fact that his listener is soon going to be a corpse, one wonders why he's wasting his breath, unless it's to give the detective time to wriggle free from his bonds, dive for the nearest weapon, and turn the tables on his captor. This device was creaky when Agatha Christie employed it in *Murder Is Easy* in 1939, yet it's still clunking along; it appeared in 1994 in Mary Higgins Clark's *Remember Me*. In each case it took a compelling story that rose well above genre and brought it down to the level of a Grade-B programmer from Hollywood's bargain basement.

Oh, but weren't those bestselling books? Without a doubt. They were also both written by proven performers who had established themselves years earlier, and who might expect their loyal readership to forgive a bit of carelessness as they rush to deadline. In these cases, the assumption is based on a kind of earned arrogance. In the case of the beginner who hopes to emulate their success, it's awkward and lazy.

INFORMATION OVERLOAD

Today, the need to avoid prolixity is greater than ever. In the 60,000-word format that set the standard for the detective novel of the 1940s through the 1970s, a lot of talk near the end was merely irritating. The 100,000-plus-word blockbuster now requested by publishers, with its longer list of suspects, compound crimes and labyrinth of subplots, counterplots and burial plots, demands so much explaining that to attempt to do it all in one scene would provide a universal cure for insomnia.

Writers who remember the 160-page novels that launched the careers of John D. MacDonald and Thomas B. Dewey are fond of mourning the loss of a length that made it easier for the reader to remember clues. In those days—not so long ago—the average adult had a lot less to remember in general than his counterpart today. The technological revolution and the breakup of the telephone company has ushered in a busload of essential information that a decade ago would have seemed like gibberish. Forced to store eleven-digit telephone numbers, nine-numeral zip codes, various PINs, a personal computer access code, and constantly shifting time slots for all his favorite television programs on cable, satellite, and proliferating broadcast networks, a reader runs the risk of overloading his memory circuits just trying to keep straight the names of the characters in a compelling mystery. Expecting him to retain all the complex details long enough to recognize the murderer when he is unmasked requires an occasional reminder.

A little past the halfway point in the forthcoming Amos Walker novel, *Never Street*, I let Walker pause in the midst of his deepening investigation into the disappearance of his client's husband, a stressed-out small-businessman with a history of emotional problems, to take stock of what he has learned and what he still needs to find out:

> . . . I sat back and thought about the Pakistani psychiatrist, brown and pleasant-looking, sitting in his green office and not discussing the nervous breakdown that had placed Neil Catalin in his care eighteen months ago. I thought about Tom Balfour, the island brat and all-around dogsbody, and his suspicions that Naheen videotaped his sessions with his patients for purposes of shaking them down . . .
>
> . . . I supposed I was indirectly responsible for Fat Phil's beating death. . . . On the other hand, if the Iroquois Heights detective hadn't tried to cash in on Webb's homicide, I wouldn't have had any reason to feel guilty. So that was one more thing to stuff into my little internal box of angst and sit on the lid until it locked.

Such introspection, coming naturally to a character of average intelligence—there is only one Sherlock Holmes, after all—increases the illusion of reality while painlessly bringing the reader up to speed. It also allows insight into the detective's personality, enabling him to express self-doubts he would never reveal in dialogue. Since no other character has this access, the reader is let in on secrets exclusive to him. It's as if a co-worker he likes and admires has entrusted him with his ATM number.

TIED UP IN KNOTS

Just as the expanded form requires the detective to take these little information breaks from time to time, so the long succession of mysteries typical to that form must be dispensed with one by one as the story progresses, rather than all at once at the end. Think of the plot as a string into which knots have been tied at intervals. The detective unties each knot as he comes to it, saving the biggest and most difficult for last.

In tying these knots, it's useful to think backwards. Say an important official in the U.S. State Department has been killed in order to conceal a crime of international proportions. Her faithless husband has been paid off and relocated to a tropical paradise to ensure his silence, taking along his mistress, who leaves her cat in a friend's safekeeping. When the cat disappears, the friend engages the detective to find it—at which point the story begins. Suspecting that the cat has returned to its owner's apartment, he breaks in and finds a recent bill for hundreds of dollars in tropical resort clothing; a mystery, since the woman had told her friend she was going to Fairbanks. Curious, he checks the airport, where a ticket clerk identifies the woman from a photograph as a passenger on a flight to Marseille. Before long the detective is on his way to the French Riviera, up to his trenchcoat collar in murder and international intrigue.

Along the way he will encounter his fair share of red herrings, dead-end leads, false assumptions and cases of mistaken identity, and it will be in the best interest of the story if he follows each one out in its turn, tidying as he goes, so that he is faced at the climax with naught but the Awful Secret that the State Department official was slain to cover up. He will also find the cat.

The cat must not be forgotten. Not because mystery readers seem to harbor an odd affinity for the species (ask Lillian Jackson Braun and Carole Nelson Douglas), but because whatever device the writer uses to involve a private operator in the public business of murder must be dealt with on its own merits. The solution to this simplest mystery can be a throwaway; the cat waltzes in through an open window while the detective is examining the sinister clothing bill. The first knot thus comes undone while he is looking for a place to start on the next. The reader is hooked, for he now knows he can trust the writer to answer all his questions. When this does not happen, and the knots begin to accumulate, so too does his sense of unease, until he lays the novel aside for something more certain, like the local TV listings.

MORE THAN THE SUM OF ITS PARTS

Mind, the story should be more than just a series of problems to be solved. That approach was appropriate for the Labors of Hercules, and no one working a crossword puzzle would thank the person who designed it for going off on tangents. But the detective novel aspires to be something more than an exercise in logic. From the beginning, the American private eye story has sought to attract audiences who read in order to increase their understanding of the world around them. If the novelist creates interesting, realistic characters, a compelling plot, plausible dialogue, and a believable setting, he has extended the confines of his genre to encompass that realm of literature that brings readers back to find out what they may have missed the first time. The cat of our generic mystery plot is more than just a handle for the hero to seize and be swept up in the story, but a living, purring, genital-licking feline, suitable for stroking or kicking off the couch. The murdered public servant is not just a corpse, but a fellow human being cut down before her time, and whose spirit cries out for justice. For all its bright bikinis and foaming surf, the Riviera of the story is a dazzling trap, seductive and fatal. To reduce all this in the penultimate scene to figures on a clicking calculator is a greater crime than the one being investigated.

For the climax to work, only one serious question should remain to be answered. This eliminates distraction and allows the reader to concentrate upon the central issue. Whether the issue is the identity of the murderer or the reason for the murder (the Awful Secret) depends upon the question the detective has returned to during each of his personal briefing sessions. Since clearing it up may involve a fair amount of talking, something must be happening in the scene—preferably something dangerous—to draw attention away from that fact.

"When in doubt," Raymond Chandler once wrote, "have a man come in through a door with a gun in his hand." A gun is a marvelous prop, so constant a symbol of death as to transcend cliché, and in the hand of the villain, where it is liable to go off at any second, it is always useful. Someone inching toward the plug of a lamp, poised to plunge the room into darkness, is equally effective. In *Angel Eyes*, Amos Walker's second book-length adventure, I shamelessly used both:

> . . . I let my eyes drop to the floor, pretending to be choosing my words. After a moment I located the cord to the lamp where it plugged into the wall. It was good to know for future reference.
>
> " . . . you kept a cool head, not forgetting to collect your father's derringer afterwards, so that your mother could carry out the plans she had for it. But you should have taken time to search his office and grab the account book he used to record DeLancey's blackmail payments."
>
> "Who'd have thought he was stupid enough to bank them?" Clendenan brought out the little Forehand & Wadsworth.
>
> I fired the .38 through my jacket pocket. He fired at the same time, but his shot went wild and shattered the front window behind me. Then he folded onto his knees and pitched forward, still holding the now-useless single-shot. His mother screamed.
>
> I didn't bother to look and see what the bodyguards were up to. Instead I twirled the lamp cord around my ankle and jerked the china-base lamp off the end table beside Janet Whiting's chair. We both hit the floor at the same time . . .

Walker does most of the talking, relieving the villain of the implausible necessity of explaining himself to his intended victim. The early introduction of the lamp cord diverts from the effect of what would otherwise be an unbroken monologue.

The scene is a three-ring circus, made up of Walker, the villain, his accomplice mother, a pair of hired thugs and a missing judge who is bleeding copiously from a critical head wound into the lap of Walker's female client. Both Earl Derr Biggers's Charlie

Chan and Rex Stout's Nero Wolfe faced similarly packed houses during the pivotal scenes in their books, but these were static gatherings, in which the sleuths held forth in detail from a fixed position while the assembled suspects fidgeted in their seats. I count myself an attentive reader, but there were occasions when, by the time the murderer's name was announced, I'd forgotten who he or she was.

Admittedly, the Stout and Biggers books are classics. They are also very much products of the time in which they debuted, when flappers and bootleggers claimed the front pages of tabloids and Depression breadlines filled newsreels. The titles continue to sell, but mostly on the basis of Charlie Chan's famous apothegms ("Only very clever man can bite pie without breaking crust") and Nero Wolfe's cozy, insular world of ironclad hours for work and pleasure, world-class meals, and prizewinning orchids rather than for the excitement of their story lines. Had these detectives made their first appearance in today's market of authentic police procedurals (where planned gatherings of suspects are counterproductive to the process of obtaining confessions) and explosive, world-in-the-balance international thrillers, the going may have been difficult. Even Tolstoy and Shakespeare would have to shade their talents to meet the competition from computer games and rock videos.

We are living in the Information Age. Stores of knowledge pour from screens, fax machines and cellular telephones, unedited and undigested, in volumes scarcely thought possible a few years ago. This is all the more reason for private eye writers to dole out data judiciously. Your books should not read as if they were dictated by a machine. They should keep the reader tied up until the last knot is unraveled, then make them want to be tied up all over again.

CREATIVITY

Writers Write!

Robert J. Randisi

Perhaps the most clichéd of all questions a writer is asked at conferences and conventions, and even during interviews, is "Where do you get your ideas?" But being a cliché actually gives the question legitimacy, so I'll try to answer it satisfactorily.

First of all it's a hard question to answer because sometimes you don't know where an idea comes from. Often they spring to mind, unbidden, and begin to ferment until you write them down somewhere. These are probably the best ideas because they come with no effort—and believe me, they do come.

However, there are times when they don't come as easily . . .

No one sits down at a typewriter or computer without an idea, so the idea must come first. Where the idea comes from varies from writer to writer, but certain ways ideas come to you are unavoidable. For instance, watching a movie or reading a book you can suddenly be struck with the thought, "Wait a minute. What if the protagonist of this book zigged instead of zagged?"

I'm not saying you could take a whole book or movie plot, rewrite it to that point and then continue on in a new direction. I'm saying that the question "What if?" asked in the midst of watching a movie or reading a book can lead you to a plot or story idea. (A story idea, by the way, is not a book. Once you have this idea, you then need to construct a plot around it. They're two different things.)

Another way of coming up with ideas is one I use quite a bit. Because I write so many books—see my bio—I often find ideas for new books while researching the book I'm working on.

By making notes that you will refer to later, when you've finished the book you're working on, you will have stockpiled ideas for future projects.

I actually asked some writers where they get their ideas and people like Ed Gorman, John Lutz and Christine Matthews said the same type of thing. To put it in the form of advice: Keep your eyes and ears open. Ideas are all around you. They're in the newspaper, they're in conversations you hear in airports and malls, in grocery stores, or casinos, or in the lobby of a hotel, or at conventions. You simply have to be open to them, and not walk around cut off from what's going on around you.

So where do you get your ideas? Real life is a hell of a research tool, which means you have to be aware of current events not only from newspaper and TV and radio newscasts, but from simple events that get the slightest coverage. I have a bulletin board in my office that is covered with small clippings from newspapers, all of which will someday find their way onto the written page.

Keep a bulletin board, or a file of index cards, or a journal, but every time an idea occurs to you, *write it down someplace.* The worst feeling in the world is getting a great idea, and then forgetting it later.

The best way, however, to generate ideas is also the way to avoid writer's block.

Write.

Write every day.

As *Writing the PI Novel* goes to publication I will have published close to 290 books since 1982. Not once during that time have I ever suffered the dreaded disease "writer's block." You see, I don't believe in it. I think writer's block is the invention of writers who don't really want to write. It's very easy to say that you're "blocked" and, therefore, not have to do a day's work—and believe me, writing is work. That is why if you want to do this for a living you do it every day, without fail. If you sit at your typewriter or word processor, or if you write longhand, doing it every single day, no matter what the weather is like, or how you feel, is the single most surefire way to guarantee you will always have ideas, and will always be able to work on them.

Keep this in mind: Writers write!

Putting Yourself on the Page

Les Roberts

Neophyte writers, most of whom have a drawer full of half-completed manuscripts and multiply-rejected first novels, frequently get themselves all worked up because they have, in their dreams or in the shower or while washing the kitchen floor, come up with what they consider to be a terrific story.

It just might be. But they invariably have bad news coming. I've read their story.

So have you, so has everyone. In the history of the written word, scholars have only been able to differentiate and isolate thirty-six different stories. And if you look closely and boil those thirty-six down, there are really only eight or nine.

The *Star Wars* trilogy, for instance, was an intergalactic remake of *Shane*, with Luke Skywalker as Brandon de Wilde, Han Solo as the mysterious gunfighter, and Darth Vader as Jack Palance. Similarly, *E.T. The Extra-Terrestrial* was really only a modernist variation on the classic and timeworn theme of a boy and his dog, except this time it was boy and his space alien. John Ford and John Wayne made the same movie over and over again. *I Love Lucy* did the same story every week for years— Lucy wanting to be in Ricky's nightclub act. Ditto *Ozzie and Harriet*, and who Rick was taking to the dance.

In the private eye genre, I don't know a single writer who doesn't acknowledge his debts to Chandler and Hammett and MacDonald each time we boot up our computers.

What on earth can you do, then, that hasn't been done before by someone else—and probably done better?

By utilizing the only thing you have to bring to the party that is unique, one-of-a-kind, and impossible for any other writer, even the great ones, to duplicate.

Yourself.

WRITE THE BOOK THAT'S UNIQUE TO YOU

That's right, yourself. Your secret weapon. Only you can write your book. I can't write it, and you can't write mine.

Any idiot can tell a story. Look, I'll prove it to you by telling one: There's this sea captain, see? And one day this big white whale comes and bites off his leg. He's so upset by this that he spends the rest of his life chasing this one whale all over the world, and when he finally finds it, it sinks his ship, killing him and everyone else on it except one guy, improbably named Ishmael, who survives to tell the tale.

Now that you've heard that story, does it mean you don't have to read *Moby Dick*? I hope not.

What makes *Moby Dick* great is the author's feelings about Captain Ahab, about life, about the existence of God or lack thereof. In the hands of anyone else—Hawthorne, for instance, or Ernest Hemingway, or you or me—it would have been a very different book indeed. Not necessarily better, or worse—but different. Because Herman Melville put himself, his values, his philosophy, his opinions, and yes, even his prejudices on the page and made that simple story of man and beast his very own.

Nobody ever confused *Moby Dick* with Peter Benchley's *Jaws*—but isn't it, when all is said and done, the same story?

And they are both valid, compelling books, no matter how foolish I feel putting the two of them in the same sentence. Each author brought himself and his view of the world to the work.

No one is suggesting for a minute that you write your autobiography and call it fiction, for God's sake! First of all, your life probably isn't nearly as fascinating to the rest of us as it is to you. Besides, you probably had to be there. And most people won't find the facts that your Great Aunt Cecile used to laugh like a vacuum cleaner and your Uncle Mortie would frequently take out his teeth at the table when the vicar was invited to dinner sufficient motivation to fork over twenty plus bucks for your novel.

But in order to write honestly and effectively you must somehow put yourself onto the page. Your beliefs, your perceptions, your particular take on life, people and situations. If you're not doing this, you're probably writing like somebody else writes. And we'd all rather read first-rate *you* than your fifth-rate imitation of somebody else. It's not by accident there's an annual literary competition called the "bad Hemingway" contest; it's because the only good Hemingway was written by Hemingway.

Sue Grafton has admitted publicly that Kinsey Millhone is really Sue Grafton, at least in the way she looks at the world. Ask Bill Pronzini, as so many do, what the Nameless Detective's real name is, and he'll tell you it's Bill Pronzini and wonder why you had to ask. I've even said that my own two fictional creations, Saxon of Los Angeles and Milan Jacovich of Cleveland, are the yin and yang of my personality. Where else can we tap the wellsprings that inform our characters if not within ourselves?

Jack London, who has been dead since 1916, recently appeared on the New *York Times* Best Seller list. His work survives because it is so uniquely his own expression of who he was and what he believed.

Of course you probably haven't lived as exciting a life as Jack London. Let's hope not, anyway—he killed himself when he was forty.

WHAT PULLS YOUR TRIGGER?

This is definitely not one of those hoary "write what you know" creeds. If we only wrote what we knew, all works of fiction would be about writers. And most of us, sad to tell, don't know all that much.

Write instead what excites you—that's the way to go. Write about what floats *your* boat, what pushes *your* buttons, and write it courageously and with passion. Bring yourself to the work, and give yourself over to it utterly so that it becomes more than a "good story," but a true personal expression, one that can't be duplicated by anyone else. When the reader finishes your novel, you should be, if not friends, at the very least close acquaintances.

Any published author will tell you that the most-asked question of them is "Where do you get your ideas?" When I'm not feeling flippant and tell them there's a little old guy in New Jersey who sells then to me nine for twenty-five bucks, I admit that I get as many as twenty new ideas every day. Ideas are the easy part—it's writing the damn book that's so hard.

But with so many ideas, why do I write the ones I choose to write? Why not the others? Because there are ideas that keep clawing inside the belly to get out—the ones that resonate in a very specific way with me. The ideas that are meaningful to me, that I want to write about and share with other people. It's a personal choice in a personal business.

Walk around with what I like to call the Writer's Eye. Observe people, places, things, eavesdrop on the conversation of strangers. Never go anywhere without a notebook or a tape recorder, and record your impressions while they're fresh.

But remember they have to be *your* impressions. It isn't enough to simply describe a character—hair color, eyes, body, clothing, etc. What's needed is how you feel about that character, and how you'd like the reader to feel about him or her. We've all seen people on the street that for some reason we'd just like to slap. Or take to bed without preamble. Or get to know. We've all been introduced to someone we'd like to spend time with, but we don't quite know why. The writer, who's looking through the Writer's Eye, knows. And lets the reader know, too.

EXPOSE YOURSELF

Wait a minute, you're saying. If I put my true fantasies down on paper, if I express my real, deep emotions, what will my mother think? How can I let my children know I have thoughts and feelings like that? What will this do to my marriage and/or my relationship? Will my neighbors duck down another supermarket aisle when they see me pushing my shopping cart toward them? Are my friends going to snicker and point? Is my boss going to be appalled? Will my clergyman denounce me from the pulpit? How can I expose myself like that?

Sorry, shy retiring violet, but that's the job. When you finish, if you don't suddenly have the uncomfortable feeling that your fly is open or your bra strap is showing, you probably didn't do it right. Writing fiction is a lot like getting naked in public. If you aren't willing to show your wrinkles and sags, if you aren't ready to allow readers to see inside you, to where you really live and who you really are, then you should forget about writing and become an accountant, a pieceworker, or one of those faceless minions who ask customers if they'd like fries with that. Find another hobby where you don't have to invest anything of yourself.

And when questioned by your friends and challenged by the people who come to see you at book signings, you can always tell them, "Hey, it's fiction." That's your escape hatch—and it's true. They'll never know which part of it you made up and which part is really the skinny. Just keep that tantalizing, enigmatic smile on your puss—it'll drive them nuts.

Besides, you're probably worrying about a situation that will never come to pass anyway. I doubt if anyone really thinks Hannibal Lecter is Thomas Harris' alter ego or that the author of *The Silence of the Lambs* ever cooked anyone's liver and ate it with fava beans. It takes a twisted mind like yours or mine to wonder about something like that.

Just relax and let the writing come out. Free yourself from all your hang-ups by letting them happen on the page.

FIND YOUR OWN VOICE

When my first book was published, an old friend read it and wrote me from Chicago that he'd felt as if he'd just spent the evening with me. It remains my favorite compliment about my work.

For those of us who know and have spent time with the wonderful Lawrence Block, the novels he writes are unmistakably his, informed with his wry wit, his sometimes through-a-glass-darkly view of human nature, his erudite manner of speaking. I could pick out a Larry Block novel in the dark—because no one writes exactly the way he does, with exactly that kind of elegance and power. And even though his two series protagonists, private eye Matthew Scudder and bookseller-cum-burglar Bernard Rhodenbarr, are very different men indeed, they both speak with the voice or voices of Lawrence Block, because he puts himself on the page so unsparingly.

I'm not a private detective and never have been. I am not Slovenian like Milan Jacovich, and I wouldn't drink his beverage of choice, Stroh's Beer, at gunpoint. He's a lot bigger than I am. I don't smoke Winstons and I never played football and my luck in things romantic is marginally better than his, thank God. But his fierce loyalty to his family and friends, his love of his home town, the pain of his divorce and being a weekend father, and his sometimes rigid, with-me-or-agin-me take on what is and is not acceptable to him, all come directly from inside me.

Saxon looks more like me, albeit younger, tougher and thinner. We both have prematurely gray hair—at least my gray hair used to be premature. He makes more money than I do; is a loner while I am an extremely social guy; is very much a creature of his Los Angeles environment, which I ran from several years ago; and is a lapsed Catholic who drags his parochial guilt around behind him like a sack. He's quick with a poke in the chops, and I haven't hit anyone in anger since I was eleven. But we're both quick to anger when confronted with bigotry, we both like beautiful women and expensive Scotch a bit more than is healthy for us, we both have a bitterly cynical outlook on the Hollywood scene, he shares my Chicago upbringing and his "backstory" is very similar to mine.

I don't just make myself the good guy, though. Frequently I will assign some of what I know to be my less endearing qualities to some of the miscreants and skels and grifters and wise guys who romp through my pages. It's therapeutic and cathartic, a way of ruefully acknowledging some of my shortcomings and, in a sense, apologizing for them. All my characters— male, female, good and evil—are parts of me, or others filtered through my brain and viscera and screened through my perceptions. How could I do otherwise?

So don't take this advisement to "put yourself on the page" literally. But invest enough of who you are in your story and your characters so that they'll ring true and honest. I know how my protagonists feel in a given situation, because in a very practical way, they are me.

MAKE STUFF UP

Let your imagination soar along with your words—that's why we get paid. But if you're going to create a private detective as a series lead, don't look for the gimmicks. We've had them all— blind PIs, gay PIs, physically handicapped PIs, married, single, divorced, alcoholic, rich, drug-addicted, cigar-smoking, piano-playing, womanizing, celibate, Jewish, Catholic, Slovenian, ago-raphobic, cat-loving, orchid growing, overweight, undersized, under-loved, highly educated, amputee, ex-athlete, ex-cop, ex-con, ex-nun, ex-actor, ex-lawyer, defrocked priest, hardboiled, bumbling, accidental, cowardly PIs. The gimmicks, good and bad, have all been taken.

Instead, think about the kind of private detective you would be, or want to be, if you weren't whatever you are. You don't have to make the character look like you or do what you do for a living. But you must infuse the character with yourself— your feelings, your politics, your tastes, your particular morality. Writing from inside, from your own truth, will give your writing the verisimilitude and honesty that will lift it above lesser and more superficial works.

Even if you write across gender—a male writer with a female protagonist or vice-versa—you still need that personal commitment. If you're a woman, don't try to figure out how a man thinks. Figure out how you would think if you were a man.

Make him yours—your creation, your literary spokesman.

Look up the job description of a novelist and you'll find it says: "Makes stuff up." It's so. I write about murders without ever having committed one. I make it up. But the make-up, the imagination, has to come from somewhere. Wherever it is, it's inside me, and makes me write the books I do instead of some other kind. The characters in my novels are, without exception, people I've seen or met or passed on the street, people who have somehow struck me in one way or another. If I didn't do that, my next book would be about my drapes, because that's what I look at all day.

I make up stories about the people I see which are mostly not true—but they are the writer's truth, and they come from who I am, what I do and what kind of mood I'm in today. If I see a woman wearing too much make-up, a man with a bad haircut, or a person with a perpetual look of astonishment on his face, I not only take notes about how they look, but about how they made me feel. Does the woman's thick cosmetic mask make me feel scornful toward her? Do I pity her pathetic attempt to make herself look younger? Does it make her seem sexier and more attractive? Do I thoughtlessly laugh at her? Those are all reactions, nice or not-so-nice, that come from me; when I transfer them to paper, I not only write what I see, but I interpret it.

You probably don't know where you're going to use these notes—or even if you will. But weeks or months or maybe even years later, you'll be writing along, ready to introduce a new character, and there she is, the make-up lady, over-rouged and big as life, and on the page the way you want her to be, because you're the writer and what you say goes.

BE MASTER OF YOUR DOMAIN

A writer is godlike at the keyboard. The characters created will do exactly as they are bid, and if they're good they are rewarded with a happily-ever-after. If not, they are punished, sometimes killed. So if you're going to write, if you're going to be godlike and giveth and taketh away and smite with plagues and be wrathful and vengeance-seeking. When you think of the biblical tale that God created man in His own image, you'll know that it's perfectly all right to create your fictional protagonist in your image, to one extent or the other.

Someone—with a giant ego—once said he could move the world if only he had a place to stand. Well, writers have to know themselves, who they are and what they stand for, because that self-knowledge is what gives them a place to stand and comment on the world of which they write, and that takes time. A good writer almost always has a personal philosophy, and he's not reticent about letting us see it shining through between the lines.

And since you'll be writing from the sense of yourself, you'll find that your work and your words take wing on the wind of your convictions.

Not that every book has to have a message. Messages are for e-mail. But if your story and your characters and the way you put words together on the page are not all reflections of yourself and what you believe in—what in hell are you writing for?

It doesn't matter who you are, where you were born, what your race or your politics—when you are reading *Gone With the Wind* you are a Rebel, rooting for the Confederacy and damning the Yankees and admiring the grace and the pathetic gallantry of the South of the nineteenth century. Margaret Mitchell, writing seventy years after the fact, put herself and her Southern sensibilities on the page and created a timeless classic. I don't know how close she was to Scarlett O'Hara, but I know how close she was to Scarlett's cause. Even in a novel of such sweeping scope and breadth, the author managed to write an intensely personal novel.

Most of us who have been fortunate enough to see our books on the shelves of the local public library write the kind of things we ourselves like to read. We don't check out the best-seller list and try to duplicate whatever is on it. We make no attempt to second-guess the market. We don't consciously set out to write the Great American Whatever, any more than John Huston and Humphrey Bogart deliberately tried to make what, fifty-five years later, is still considered the best detective film ever. We endeavor to make our own personal statement, in our own personal, inimitable way. How we think, what we believe, the way we see it.

That's what you, as fledgling writers, must do too. It isn't your job to compare your work to Hammett or Chandler or Dorothy B. Hughes. It's your job to Do It! Just Do It! Write the best you know how—honestly, without flinching, without imposing some false, phony style or plot or template that even a casual reader will be able to spot by page two. Put yourself in it; let us see what you're made of.

Sure, plot is important. Sure, style is important. Sure, all the things you've heard in dozens of writer's conferences and seminars and everything you've read in articles like this one—it's all important.

But the most essential thing of all to a writer, in my opinion, is that mantra we used to yell at our kids in Little League, imploring them not to swing at a bad pitch but to wait for a good one: "Make it be yours."

Write well.

Writing and Reading

Ed Gorman

Ernest Hemingway once noted that great writers don't borrow—they steal. What he was saying, of course, is that in the course of reading the fiction of others you find all sorts of goodies that you can use in your own fiction.

A few years ago I taught a summer writing course. I had a good time. The students were bright, friendly and eager to learn.

One of the first questions I asked them was how much time they put aside each day for writing. This was a very hip class. Each student made time to write each and every day.

Then I asked them how much time they set aside for reading.

Not one of the sixteen made time for reading. Several of them said that with all their various commitments, there just wasn't much time for reading.

To me, reading is an integral part of writing.

When I first set out to write a mystery novel, I started outlining every mystery I read. Nothing elaborate, you understand. But I'd write a sentence or two about each chapter. After I did this enough times I began to see the mechanics of how a mystery novel is put together. The whole progress of writing mysteries became a lot less . . . mysterious.

While I'd had problems actually finishing a novel, when I finally did the deed, I wrote every morning for seventy days straight and I sold my first novel to the first editor who saw it. I credit much of my success to all the reading I did.

I still read at least two mystery or suspense novels a week.

I always will. Some may consider this checking out the competition . . . but I'm more inclined to see it as studying the way a student does: to learn.

READ TO LEARN

A few years ago I read a Ruth Rendell novel that made me look at interior monologue in a completely new way. I'd been planning a book about child movie stars for a long time but could never find the right voice to launch it. Reading Rendell gave me the voice and the technique I'd been looking for. Now, if I were to give you both Rendell's novel and my own, you probably wouldn't see many similarities at all. While I borrowed from her, I made my material very much my own. But if I hadn't read the Rendell novel, I doubt I'd have found my starting point and my book *Shadow Games* might still be unwritten.

Ed McBain is another suspense writer whose books have taught me a great deal. McBain (Evan Hunter) is the first to admit that he breaks many of the rules . . . and that's why his books are usually so fresh and lively. He shifts tenses, intrudes as author upon the narrative, introduces comedic moments in the middle of breakneck melodrama, and even solves mysteries that took place four or five books back in the series. I suspect he does all these things to keep himself from getting bored, and it certainly keeps his readers from being bored, too.

McBain is worth studying in depth. Note how he gets in and out of scenes. He uses a variety of hooks and devices that keeps the reader constantly flipping pages. Many of his books are driven by dialogue. Erle Stanley Gardner was a master at using dialogue to tell his story, too, but McBain is a better writer, and he is also a more serious student of the human dilemma than Gardner was.

For plotting, I've spent dozens of hours looking at the books of Marcia Muller. In her usual self-effacing manner, Marcia insists that her early books are less than wonderful. Don't believe her. Those first few books of hers are great introductions to how mysteries are told. To be sure, her later books are richer, more resonant and more complicated than her earlier books. But nonetheless *Edwin of the Iron Shoes* and *Ask the Cards a Question* taught me a great deal about the mystery form. I still reread them from time to time.

One rainy Sunday afternoon I was worrying about my current novel, which was due in sixty days. I'd had several false starts and ended up throwing away more than two hundred pages. I was feeling desperate.

I went downstairs to my library and started looking through my mystery collection. Somebody had recently sent me a Donald E. Westlake novel titled *Murder Among Children*, which Don had done under the name Tucker Coe. This was Westlake's series about a New York City cop who was not there when his partner needed him. The partner died. In addition to being a powerful novel of character, *Children* rewards readers with an intriguing look at the flower power revolution of the sixties. You sense that the narrator, who is in his forties, doesn't approve of hippies but he makes some remarkable (and even-handed) observations about hippies nonetheless, turning the book into a fascinating social document as well.

I read the book in two hours, sat down and wrote out the plot, and then started looking back through the book. It is a marvel of construction, style and character. It is one of the most perfectly wrought mystery novels I've ever read. The book I wanted to write was nothing like it but I found myself so inspired by Westlake's brilliance that it carried me through my own writing. *New Improved Murder*, my book, sold to paperback reprint, two book clubs and three foreign publishers. It has also been optioned three times as a film. I've always felt that I owed a lot of this, in a very real sense, to Don Westlake. I've been reading him since I was fifteen years old—which is something like thirty years now—and I've probably learned more from him than any other author I've ever read. Pound for pound (or page for page, I suppose I should say) Westlake is probably the best crime writer of his generation.

That's another reason I read. If I read a good book, then

I'll be more likely to write well myself. And I don't mean just mysteries. I read a lot of mainstream fiction (I'm currently reading through the novels of Robert Stone) and even spend time with poetry. I'm presently rereading a lot of Frost and Auden. For me, poetry will always be the most exalted of human expressions, and it's nice to get a rush from it every once in a while. You know, the way we used to get a rush back in the sixties from those substances that Bill Clinton says he didn't inhale.

READ FOR IDEAS

One final reason to read a lot: The fiction of other people can give you a lot of ideas for your own use. The late western author Max Brand used to read half a novel and then set it down and plot out the second half himself. Then he had the outline for a new novel of his own. Now this is a little mechanical and bloodless for my tastes—not to mention legally risky—but I certainly understand the process. Half the stories I've written have come from a character or a plot turn or phrase I read in someone else's work. So, I not only enjoy my reading, I also find it useful.

SUGGESTED READING

I'm going to end this by listing twenty-five suspense novels that I've found particularly stimulating to read and reread over the years. I'm not saying that these are the absolute best, but I am saying you will be richly rewarded by reading these books at least once, and then spending some time studying them.

Brighton Rock, by Graham Greene
A Kiss Before Dying, by Ira Levin
The Chill, by Ross Macdonald
The Far Side of the Dollar, by Ross Macdonald
The Long Goodbye, by Raymond Chandler
How Like an Angel, by Margaret Millar
Whispers, by Dean Koontz
The Killer Inside Me, by Jim Thompson
The So-Blue Marble, by Dorothy B. Hughes

The 31st of February, by Julian Symons
The Far Cry, by Fredric Brown
Pity Him Afterwards, by Donald E. Westlake
Blue Lonesome, by Bill Pronzini
The Lake of Darkness, by Ruth Rendell
The Body in the Library, by Agatha Christie
Before the Fact, by Frances Iles
Phantom Lady, by Cornell Woolrich
Goldilocks, by Ed McBain
The End of the Night, by John D. MacDonald
Wolf in the Shadows, by Marcia Muller
After the First Death, by Lawrence Block
Kill the Boss Goodbye, by Peter Rabe
A Time of Predators, by Joe Gores
Falling Angel, by William Hjortsberg
The Murder of Miranda, by Margaret Millar

I hope you'll excuse me now. I've enjoyed talking about all these great books so much I'm going to take one down from the shelf and read it.

CHARACTER

Developing a Series Character

Jeremiah Healy

I've written eleven novels in the John Francis Cuddy series, from the first, *Blunt Darts*, in 1984, to the most recent, *Invasion of Privacy*, in 1996. I've also contributed articles and delivered lectures on mystery writing. For a perspective here on developing a series character, let's borrow some concepts from the realm of military science.

Most of us have heard the expressions "strategy" and "tactics." As rough definitions, assume that strategy represents the long-term plan for winning a war, while tactics represent the short-term plan for winning a battle. If each book is a battle (and even relatively peace-loving writers might endorse that metaphor), then an author generally can change any or all of his or her tactics from book to book. For example, you can alter the way you write dialogue or the manner in which you describe settings.

Happily you can change most of your strategy from book to book as well, including the way you structure a plot (e.g., linear versus flashback as the method of telling the reader the story). However, in developing a series character over a number of novels, you may discover that some apparently "tactical" decisions about your series character, perhaps reached rather casually (and even unconsciously) in book number 1 or 2, boomerang on you as unfortunate "strategic" decisions by book number 5. And, as discussed beautifully by Robert Dahlin throughout his article "In Crime, a Series in the Best M.O." (*Publishers Weekly*, vol. 241, number 13—March 28, 1994), most editors want a series with "legs"—a series that can carry the author and character(s) a long way with readers.

Accordingly, let me examine some strategic and tactical aspects of your series character, aspects for you to consider when sitting down to write the first few books featuring him or her. The following thoughts are considerations and recommendations, not hard and fast rules. As we go along, I'll try to illustrate most points with examples from mystery fiction, especially using my own and other private investigator novels. Lastly, I want to stress that reasonable minds can differ with my conclusions and even the descending order of importance I suggest in treating the aspects themselves.

PROFESSIONAL INVESTIGATOR VS. AMATEUR SLEUTH

If you're a big fan of *Murder, She Wrote*, you probably should (as the standardized-testing folks would say) move on to the next item. However, before deciding which type of protagonist your series character will be, you might learn from an experience shared with me by Linda Barnes. In her Michael Spraggue series, the main character was an independently wealthy actor and amateur sleuth. A few books into the series, however, Linda found that it was becoming increasingly difficult to believably involve Spraggue in murders, often having to "burn" five or six chapters of foundation "business" before the story—the suspense—could really build. She also had to choose as credible victims (and therefore eliminate from future books) family or friends of the protagonist.

Beginning the Carlotta Carlyle series, Linda discovered that having a professional private investigator allowed her to launch the "mystery" in chapter one, because we all can understand someone, even a total stranger, bringing a crime-laden problem to a licensed investigator. Linda gave Carlyle a "day job" as a cab driver to round out the character, but the choice of professional over amateur as to the investigating side made the effort of writing each new book in the series a lot more bearable. Therefore, my first strategic recommendation would be to cast as your series character a person who would have some professional interest in criminal investigation (see discussion under "Background" on page 84).

NARRATIVE: FIRST PERSON VS. THIRD PERSON

Looking at mystery fiction in general, I'm not sure there's a preference for either first person narration (principal character speaking to the reader as *I* or *me*) or third person narration (author speaking to the reader through a principal character as *he* or *she*). In private investigator fiction, the tradition has been to use first person (e.g., Raymond Chandler's Philip Marlowe or Ross Macdonald's Lew Archer), though there are some notable third person books (Dashiell Hammett's *The Maltese Falcon* with Sam Spade.)

One advantage of the first person narrative is the way the reader is engaged as an intimate "companion" of the series character: The entire story is told through the narrator's point of view. Another plus is that some plots are easier to "sell" to the reader because he or she understands that nothing can be "tipped," except that which the first person narrator knows. This advantage carries a concomitant disadvantage for the author, however: The way in which the story is told becomes dictated by the sequence in which the first person narrator can obtain information. Alternating chapter-to-chapter which character does the "first person" narration can temper this limitation, but the "varying first person" strategy is very difficult to execute. In fact, Dick Lochte's *Sleeping Dog*—in which the author alternates between a grizzled, fiftyish male "investigator" and an early teen, female "client"—is the only successful example I can recall.

A second disadvantage of the first person narrative is that most of us as writers tend to identify somewhat with "our" first person protagonist as an alter ego, the "person we would be" if we could. This tendency creates a tremendous temptation toward self-indulgence, to exaggerate eccentricities as virtues or to stand on soapboxes and thereby interrupt the flow of the story for the reader.

By contrast, the third person approach allows for a greater—and perhaps healthier—distance between author and main character. Also, the third person narrative provides more flexibility in sequencing the story. Elmore Leonard doesn't write "series characters" per se, but using the third person, he is able to tell the story to the reader through the varying viewpoints (and therefore voices) of the major characters in his novels. However, the third person voice requires greater authenticity and research by the author, since he or she usually can't satisfy the reader with just a first person copout ("It looked like an AK-47 to me").

Strategically, I believe the pros and cons of first person versus third person narration balance each other out, with neither approach a clear winner for all situations. Tactically, some of us who write first person narrators, like William Tapply in his Brady Coyne series or me in my John Cuddy books, have experimented with third person prologues. This device introduces the reader to a given story from an omniscient view the first person character couldn't enjoy. While the third person prologue is a good thing to do once or twice as an exercise for stretching the writer, I wouldn't rely on it as a constant crutch because I think it can become tiresome for the faithful, long-time reader.

Finally, it is possible, once you've established a series character, to "switch" him or her from first person to the third person, or vice versa, but I think this is generally confusing for the reader and appears disjointed to the editor. The masterful John Lutz has managed to pull off such a switch in his Alo Nudger series. However, he's John Lutz, and the rest of us aren't.

GENDER/ETHNICITY/SEXUAL ORIENTATION

I list these aspects together, and as only third level considerations, because I think they've become basically immaterial.

Either gender, all ethnicities, and most sexual orientations are now perfectly acceptable for a series character (though it's probably still best to avoid inter-species love.)

I do believe, however, that you should stick with your own "aspects" for all three. Take gender as an illustration: P.D. James (a woman) has done a wonderful job with her male protagonist Adam Dalgleish, and M.D. Lake (a man) has done a wonderful job with his female protagonist Peggy O'Neill. Nevertheless, it's hard to write an entire series while completely "reversing field." On the other hand, it is appropriate, and perhaps even essential, to create *supporting* characters in the series who are different to you. And, in a "one-shot" or "stand-alone" thriller, such as Teri White's brilliant *Triangle*, even three main characters of the opposite gender are maintainable. But, for the protagonist in your first series, I'd stay a little bit more with who you are until you've acquired the hang of writing novels overall.

One strategic hint in this regard: Try choosing a real person, or perhaps a composite of real people, as your main character. In my series, for example, the John Cuddy character is a combination of my dad (a military police captain during World War II) and my uncle (an insurance investigator after the war). By being able to picture a composite of these two men I grew up knowing, I can keep the "voice" and "character" of John Cuddy consistent, chapter by chapter, book after book, without a lot of time spent "researching" the prior statements and behavior of my own protagonist.

BACKGROUND

Typically, private investigators in fiction previously have been in the military (such as Mickey Spillane's Mike Hammer) or law enforcement, either directly (such as Sue Grafton's Kinsey Millhone, a former police officer) or derivatively (such as Robert B. Parker's Spenser, a former investigator for the prosecutor's office.) Also fair game in recent years are past-life reporters (Arthur Lyons's Jacob Asch) and disbarred lawyers (Stephen Greenleaf's John Marshall Tanner.)

As with the aspects of gender, ethnicity and sexual orientation discussed above, I believe that the background of your series character should parallel your own experiences as closely as possible. I was a trial attorney for five years, and issues from my earlier cases have driven many of my later novels (the tragedy of the battered wife in *Swan Dive*; the jeopardy of the reporter's confidential source in *Yesterday's News*). In order to credibly explain those issues to readers through "Cuddy's" first person narration, I gave him a year of law school. Also, Cuddy and I were both military police lieutenants during the Vietnam era, but unlike my protagonist, I was never posted overseas. To patch that strategic "hole," I've read twelve books on the war, and a friend who served two tours in-country proofreads all of the Vietnam references, just to make sure I don't make a research-reasonable (but real-world-horrible) gaffe in those passages. Back in the states and more tactically, I even have Cuddy drive the same cars I've owned or rented, so the first person impression and familiarity will come through to the reader.

Alternatives to using your own experiences require far more exhaustive research than my "hole-patching" involves. You also will need awfully good friends (or a highly compensated consultant) to vet the entirety of every manuscript for technical, experiential errors that go beyond the ken of the average copyeditor.

GROWTH/STASIS

Strategically, do you want your character to "grow" as a person from book to book or stay "static" throughout the series? Several subsidiary aspects are involved here.

The Character Himself or Herself

Many readers of Agatha Christie's Miss Marple or Rex Stout's Nero Wolfe prefer the way the character never changes, a sort of ageless traveler through the decades. Speaking with current readers, though, I believe the reason they come back to Jerome

Dolittle's Tom Bethany or Sara Paretsky's V.I. Warshawski or my John Cuddy is precisely because those characters seem more real when they change over time, hopefully in a positive, "personality maturing" way.

Aging the Character

Most of us can produce only one novel in a series per calendar year. A writer who could produce more is discouraged by his or her publisher for fear that two books in a series per year will "compete with themselves" for bookseller shelf space and book customer attention. However, even at just one novel a year, a protagonist presumably would age pretty quickly. My Cuddy character, a college grad during the Tet Offensive in 1968, would have to be nearly fifty now in a literal, chronological progression.

However, I've taken a "strategy" page from Marcia Muller, who has aged her Sharon McCone character only a few weeks or months, book to book, and thus preserves some "youthfulness" for the facets of the character that require related physical characteristics. There's nothing wrong, though, with introducing the consequences of aging into individual books, as I've done with subplots of the Cuddy character running the Boston Marathon in *Right to Die* or starting to lose some physical prowess due to injury in *Act of God*.

Love Life

This is different, it seems to me, from the previously discussed "sexual orientation." Regardless of orientation, will your main character be sexually promiscuous (nearly cartoonish in this time of AIDS), "averagely available" or completely monogamous? In my first novel, Cuddy survives a war zone only to lose his young wife, Beth, to cancer back in the states. In much the same way that my dad or uncle would have behaved, John remains faithful to her memory until he meets a young prosecutor, Nancy Meagher, who he thinks can become the next woman in his life. However, I introduced the Meagher character in just the second Cuddy novel, *The Staked Goat*. While Nancy was essential to the plot of that book, I think in hindsight I made a genuine mistake in series strategy. I should have left John a sympathetic widower for a longer period of time (i.e., a few more books) before giving him new hopes for the future. This approach would have produced better subplots in which the reader could really wonder whether a new (or reappearing) female character in a given book could evolve into his next love.

Supporting Cast

Whether your main character grows or stays static, how do you handle the supporting cast around him or her? Some supporting but continuing characters are helpful, even if they aren't central to a given novel's plot. I have a fairly small cast in the Cuddy series: the aforementioned Nancy Meagher; an African-American homicide lieutenant named Robert Murphy; an irascible newspaper reporter named Mo Katzen; and a Lebanese fitness instructor named Elie. However, Joan Hess tells me that she has such a large supporting cast in one of her series that she has to spend a great deal of time in each succeeding book just accounting for where these satellite characters are and what they are doing in their own lives. This can become difficult for the reader as well as cumbersome for the writer.

SOFT-, MEDIUM- OR HARDBOILED?

I think the answer to this question for the author beginning his or her first series is a second question: Which kind of book do you as a reader like best? Maybe you can write what you yourself enjoy reading, but even if you can't, you'll enjoy trying.

To me, a great deal of the debate on this aspect of a series character turns on the violence/humor divergence. A few people can write truly humorous books that are also believably violent. Though not series books, Carl Hiaasen's work comes to mind. Others can write books with a protagonist who is wise-guy funny and involved with homicidal violence without actually committing any of his or her own. For example, Loren Estleman has told me that his protagonist Amos Walker has never taken a life; Loren's series is so well written, I didn't remember that aspect jumping out jarringly during my prior reading of all the Walker books.

As a general matter, however, humor dilutes violence, and violence tramples humor. One way to avoid the problem is by dividing it. Lawrence Block writes two very different series, the darkly violent Matthew Scudder novels and the lighter, caperish Bernard ("Burglar") Rhodenbarr series.

Regardless of which kind of main character you choose, someone will raise a question of political correctness in whatever humor you do introduce. A tactical hint toward minimizing such criticism grows from the difference between being politically correct and demographically accurate: Give tasteless or offensive jokes to an obnoxious supporting character in your books who might credibly (though not admirably) tell such jokes, and then have your series character be offended by them.

SETTING
Historical vs. Contemporary

Series with protagonists set in historical times are quite hot now, as evidenced by the late Ellis Peters and the Brother Cadfael books set in medieval England, or Lindsey Davis and the Marcus Didius Falco books set in ancient Rome. However, strategic authenticity problems abound here, and you are stuck tactically with certain historical events and limitations (for example, does it matter to your plot when the camera or the wristwatch—or even the ballpoint pen—was invented?).

A contemporary book is easier to "research," but an authenticity problem becomes more apparent to more people when you do make a mistake. Also, you can be stuck by even "current" events and limitations: the personal radios patrol officers wear on their tunics; DNA testing available to prosecutors; faxes accessible to almost everyone. And, unlike the historical writer who knows what happens a few years beyond the story's running time, the author of a contemporary story might be frustrated or scooped by near-future revolutions no one could predict (think about what the fall of the Berlin Wall must have done to espionage works-in-progress). Anticipating the "tide," I've learned how to go online not because I had a burning desire to surf the Net but rather because I felt I had to understand virtual technology in order to have most of my characters sounding real a few years from now.

Geographic
ACTUAL VS. FICTIONAL

If you place your series character in an actual geographic setting, as I've put John Cuddy in Boston, then you have to know whether Main Street in that location runs north/south or east/west. More exactly, Robert Randisi's Miles Jacoby operates in metropolitan New York City and Benjamin Schutz's Leo Haggerty in metropolitan Washington, DC. Bob has to get the subway lines and stops right, and Ben the exits and ramps off the Beltway, or the informed reader's investment in their novels will be forfeit.

A desire for more flexibility in setting has led many authors to create fictional towns, as Nancy Pickard has done with Port Frederick in her Jenny Cain series. Even if you do create a fictional setting, however, you must keep a kind of "logs and lines" of that location, so that if Main Street in Book no. 1 did run north/south, nobody in Book no. 4 will drive east/west on it.

Finally, while I'm obviously not giving legal advice in this article, there are also a lot of potential liability traps for the unwary author in setting a fictional work about police corruption or hospital malpractice in a "real-world" town or institution. Bluntly, a writer can be sued for things he or she thought were merely make-believe.

URBAN/SUBURBAN/RURAL

Any of these settings is perfectly acceptable, but each carries with it strategic opportunities and restrictions. Cities offer diversity of architecture, people, professions, etc., while small towns can have better "generational" plots because everyone has lived near each other for so many years. Suburbs are often helpfully anonymous for the series character and can be captured generically in a way readers can picture.

Setting in this sense might also serve to tactically personalize the mysteries you write. Brendan DuBois can do things with the seedy New Hampshire seacoast resort in his Lewis Cole series that would require my protagonist to face a "fish-out-of-water" plot, as I've tried in *Foursome* (city boy Cuddy investigating a triple homicide at a Maine lake) and *Rescue* (New Englander Cuddy searching for a missing boy in the Florida Keys). On the other hand, I can have my series character take a one-hour drive and be in any one of three different states while James Crumley must build a Rocky Mountain auto odyssey of eight hours or so into a plot line for Milo Milodragovitch to reach a major city.

CONCLUSION

There are many aspects to consider in developing your series character, and nobody can prescribe the subjective "magic" that will make any contributing "hero" a success as well. However, this discussion of at least some of those aspects may help you strategically and tactically to plan that series better, perhaps even to realize that the book you want to write really should be a one-shot or stand-alone novel rather than the debut of a series character. In the end though, probably the best advice is the simplest: Sit down and write the book you want to write with the protagonist you want to project. If readers enjoy your principal character, editors will encourage you to turn him or her into a frequent visitor to your computer screen.

The PI's the Thing

Robert J. Randisi

O kay, it's a play on words, but the immortal Bard never created a PI, or he wouldn't have said, "The play's the thing."

You see, in PI fiction it's the PI who carries the story, who is the "thing," and not the other way around. You can have the greatest story, the greatest plot, the most wonderful ending in the world, but if you're readers do not find your PI appealing, likeable, interesting—one, two or all three—you're going to lose them.

There are other articles in this book concerned with characterization, or creating a series character. I'm not talking about that. Whether your character is meant to be a series character or the star of a one-shot novel, my point is the same. The reader either has to like him, or find him interesting, to continue reading.

THE SERIES PI

What I'm discussing here, more than anything else, is the PI novel where the private eye is virtually on every page. This is usually told in a first person narrative, but there are cases where, while the story is being told in the third person, it might as well be first. A perfect example of this kind of book, or series, is John Lutz's Nudger series. Nudger is on every page, just as Bill Pronzini's Nameless is on every page of his novels. Nudger is told in third person, Nameless in first, and yet they're virtually the same type of book—the type that depends heavily on the lead character.

Ask any reader of PI fiction and I'll bet 90 percent of them will tell you they're more concerned with what's happening with

Nameless and his new wife Kerry than they are with Nameless's new job; or, as in the case of Jerry Healy's John Francis Cuddy, they're looking forward to Cuddy's next conversation with his dead wife rather than the next problem he's hired to solve. The same can be said for Bob Crais's Elvis Cole, Les Roberts's Milan Jacovich, Robert Parker's Spenser, or Sue Grafton's Kinsey Millhone. The people who read these books regard these characters as old friends, and they're eager to see what's happening in their lives in the next book. If they weren't eager, they wouldn't buy the next book, no matter how interesting the plot sounded. You see, it's my firm opinion that a weak plot can be carried by a strong character, but a strong plot will not support a weak character.

Stepping outside the PI genre for a moment and even stepping into TV, for an example, take the British TV series *Cracker*. The character of Fitz, with his gambling, drinking and sardonic personality, is what attracts the viewers to every show—not the case he happens to be working on. They want to see how he's going to screw up next!

Another non-PI example would be the *Inspector Morse* series. I don't read a lot of British police procedural, but I watch Morse because I like the character; I watch *Inspector Frost* because of the character. (An argument could be made here for the actor, but he *is* portraying a character, isn't he?)

Take Liza Cody's Anna Lee series. The books are very popular, but the *Anna Lee* TV series didn't quite capture the public's fancy because of the portrayal of the character. Viewers I have spoken to just didn't like the character as she appeared in the TV series.

Back to books: Janet Evanovich's Stephanie Plum books *One for the Money* and *Two for the Dough* have received praise not so much for her plotting, but for her character. Stephanie is described in a *Publishers Weekly* (*PW*) review of *Two for the Dough* as "sassy, and brassy." The reviewer went on to say that readers would likely stay ahead of the sleuthing in the book, but lauded Stephanie's affectionate relationship with her family.

Wendi Lee surrounds her PI, Angela Matelli, with brothers and sisters and a mother who knows more than she lets on, and turns even the best plotted novel into something more special by doing this. Granted, there are times when Angela's siblings get on her nerves—and the reader's—but this simply makes Angela that much more of a sympathetic character, because anyone with brothers and/or sisters can relate to her.

Michael Z. Lewin's Lunghi series introduced a family of PIs and draws the reader into their private and public lives. About the first novel, *Family Business*, *PW* said that the Lunghis were a real pleasure, goes on to describe each of them, and says they are full of promise. It spoke more of character than plot, because it is the relationship of three generations of Lunghis living in the same house, and working together as PIs, that will drive this series—if the first book is any indication.

There are other ways to make a character likeable and sympathetic than showing the reader their families.

A prime example of an author hooking the reader with her character is Sandra Scoppetone's Lauren Laurano. In the most recent novel *Let's Face the Music and Die* she offers the reader the chance to get to know her character better as Lauren's personal life takes center stage. At once she is a hunter, tracking a killer; the hunted, being stalked; and an uneasy lover, as she is tempted to stray from a longtime monogamous relationship. Through her reactions to all three of these situations the reader is given more insight than ever before into her character. This continues to be one of the more satisfying of recent PI series.

Author Jerry Keneally is also a real-life PI. While his PI Nick Polo certainly has a private life, one of the more interesting aspects of the series is knowing that Polo's methods are tried and true and based on Jerry's own real-life methods. This makes Polo infinitely more interesting than many of the fictional PIs of the past, who have relied on less realistic ways of doing things.

As for characters who might be interesting, while not exactly likeable, what of Andrew Vachss's Burke? Not exactly the ideal role model for a series PI, Burke is nevertheless a fascinating character whose sometimes lawless methods and sensibilities hold Vachss's readers breathless.

Robert B. Parker's Spenser has been known to bend the law a time or two. He's even been known to orchestrate a scenario by which he can simply blow away the bad guy, but it is his very willingness to do this for his client—or because of his own somewhat unique moral code—that draws readers to him even during a lean time when perhaps his books were not, er, exactly well plotted. (I'm told those times are gone.)

And, of course, another way to make your character appealing is to give him a sidekick who, while perhaps not exactly "appealing," certainly adds something to the mix. The aforementioned Vachss, Parker and Bob Crais have done this with their PIs' sidekicks Max the Silent, Hawk and Joe Pike. Little is known about all three of these men, except for the fact that they would do almost anything out of loyalty and yes, even affection, for Burke, Spenser and Elvis Cole.

Loren D. Estleman's Amos Walker has appealed to readers for years due to his "code" of behavior, which is perhaps most likened to that of a Raymond Chandler's Phillip Marlowe. Walker rarely, if ever, steps outside the law, and is perhaps a forties PI in a nineties world.

THE ONE-SHOT PI

I've heard a term used quite a lot lately to describe a non-series book: "one-off."

Perhaps the most famous "one-off" PI is Dashiell Hammett's Sam Spade. Aside from three short stories, Spade's only appearance was in perhaps Hammett's most famous novel, *The Maltese Falcon*. Of course, the argument can be made that the book spawned three film versions, the most famous featuring Humphrey Bogart in the role of Spade, but the book stands alone and strong on Hammett's depiction of Spade. Sometimes immoral, extremely loyal, Spade is the classic "one-off" detective. Carrying the book on his shoulders, keeping the readers turning the pages to see what he'll do about Bridget, how he'll avenge his partner—who he didn't like very much, and with whose wife he was sleeping—Spade makes *The Maltese Falcon*; the Maltese Falcon does not make Spade.

By comparison, I believe the movie versions of *The Thin Man* made the character memorable, not Hammett's single novel about Nick and Nora Charles. I have never found Nick Charles to be the kind of detective character who could carry a novel the way Sam Spade did.

Spade, at least in the beginning of the book, is not especially likeable, but he's interesting. Later we discover his moral code, after his partner is killed. To paraphrase Spade's famous speech, it doesn't matter whether you like your partner or not; when somebody kills him you're supposed to do something. This hooks the reader. You want to see if Spade succeeds in avenging his partner, and when he sends Bridget O'Shaughnessy over for it—the woman he supposedly loves—then ya gotta like him.

◆ ◆ ◆

There you have some examples of ways to make your PI an interesting and/or likeable character. He has to have some sort of code he lives by, whether it be Amos Walker's or Burke's, as long as he makes it his own, and he keeps to it.

Surround your PI with family, give him or her a loyal sidekick, keep the investigating methods interesting, and make his or her private life as much a part of the story as his or her public one. Make the reader privy to as much of the PI's character as possible. Let us know what your PI likes to eat or drink or read, what movies your PI likes, what kind of clothes he or she wears. We don't have to go to the bathroom with your character, but at least let us know that he or she goes.

The Private Eye: Doing It in Public

William L. DeAndrea

The private eye has an old and venerable history. Older and more venerable than most of us think. Up until a very short time ago, if we were talking about the earliest private eye stories, I'd slide on past Sherlock Holmes, the world's first consulting detective pulling Gregson and Lestrade's chestnuts out of the fire for a fee, of course, on back to Wilkie Collins's Sergeant Cuff in *The Moonstone.* Cuff is an official policeman, but it was apparently legal (and customary) for cops to take an agreed-upon backhander from the crime victim to whom he was devoting his talents.

Then the conversation would slip forward to the mid-1920s with Carroll John Daly's "Knights of the Open Palm" and Dashiell Hammett's first Continental Op stories.

But I haven't gone back far enough. I should have gone way back, all the way back. To the third and best of Edgar Allan Poe's C. Auguste Dupin stories, "The Purloined Letter."

The Poe stories are conceded to be the first stories devoted to a character solely because of his skill at bringing criminal secrets to light. In those three stories, plus two others not featuring Dupin, Poe created the locked room, the worshipful sidekick, the pure armchair detective, and much, much more.

And, as a closer look at "The Purloined Letter" will show, he gave us (as far as I've been able to determine) the first depiction of a detective negotiating for dough to solve a case. It is given, in fact, quite a bit of play in the story.

Monsieur G—, Prefect of Police, says he personally would double the reward offered for the recovery of the document stolen by the Minister D— (apparently, these guys stole in order to buy themselves last names). Dupin gets him to up the ante, gets the Prefect on the record with it, then produces the document and collects.

Of course, Dupin is not an official private investigator. He's not even an *un*official private investigator. In a world in which an organized governmental police force was a daring new idea, Dupin could have no PI license. The very idea would be absurd.

The idea of the PI license in reality, and in fiction, came much later.

WELCOME TO . . . FANTASY SHINGLE

It's one of the most appealing fantasies in the whole PI genre. It's been done with greater (some of our better writers) or lesser (countless B-movie Hollywood hacks) skill, but it's been seen (and enjoyed) by fans of the genre for generations.

Our brash young hero (or, in recent days, heroine), having decided to do something exciting and/or useful, supervises the hanging of his or her new shingle announcing the availability of this new purveyor of PI skills.

Before lunch those skills are hired for their first test—a beautiful widow wants to know if her boyfriend killed her husband, or if the husband faked his own death to get at the two of them. Or it might be some other dangerous or exciting situation. In any case, off we go.

Well, actually, no we don't. Not in reality. Not for almost forty years. And since the heightened illusion of reality is one of the things the PI genre prides itself on, I think we ought to be a little careful how we tread here.

It's not just a matter of hanging up a shingle. In the first place there is the matter of required experience. Throughout the U.S., states have these rules; they don't vary all that widely.

In New York, for instance, PIs must work three years in one of the following positions: police detective; police officer at or above the rank of sergeant; military police; agent in the FBI or other federal enforcement organization; or employment as a registered operative of a licensed private investigator.

This qualifies you to *apply* for a PI license. The application is followed by an investigation of you, personally, in even more detail, especially if you want a gun permit for yourself or for your agency.

Once you pass these tests, you're almost home. First, though, you have to post a bond with the state. The last time I checked it was twenty thousand dollars in New York State. It's probably a lot more now.

This bond is forfeited if you or *any of your operatives* is determined to have done something illegal. Writers take note. I don't think I've ever read a story wherein the PI is worried about losing his license because of some dumb trick one of the ops may have pulled.

And "illegal" in this case doesn't just mean failure to curb your dog, or jay-walking, or anything a regular citizen might do. It means any of the things that apply more or less exclusively to PIs.

For instance, here's one that popped my eyes open when I learned about it. PIs in the state of California may not investigate homicides. May *not*, without the permission of the police.

I was staggered. The Continental Op, with his double-digit homicide books; Philip Marlowe counting the corpses along the mean streets; Lew Archer, with his forty-year-old-murder pyramids. They may have been legal at the time, but nothing like them could happen again, unless the police attitude changes drastically.

WHAT'S A WRITER TO DO?

Well, it's certainly not the time to hoist a white flag. Now that you know some of the inconvenient facts, it should be easy enough to write around them. A simple remark from the hero about being glad to be out of the divorce-evidence mill after three years and able to do the kind of work he wants should work. A gripe about scraping up the bond would probably be enough, as well.

And if you want to know how to get around the California homicide ban, or even to use it as a plot point, read Bill Pronzini who, along with Ellery Queen (classic cozy) and Ed McBain (police procedural), has explored the limits of his chosen subgenre better than anyone in history.

But suppose a certain amount of idealism and naivete is essential to your character, that your story won't work right unless it's a first major investigation, and, moreover, that the protagonist is on his or her own.

Now what?

Big heresy coming up. How important is that shingle? How important is that PI license at all?

MCDONALD'S, KFC AND YOU

Because what we're doing, as writers, is telling a story as entertainingly, as skillfully and as plausibly as we can, we don't need a license. What we need is a *franchise*—an excuse, acceptable to the reader, to meddle in someone else's business.

Plausibility requires this, and a PI license serves admirably when it suits the story. It just doesn't always fit.

This is probably a good opportunity to discuss the whole question of franchise. A plurality of crime fiction is solved by someone who has governmental police powers, or by a close friend or relative of someone who does. There have been a notable few examples of books or whole series making comic capital out of "busybody detectives" who flout the whole idea of having to have an excuse to meddle in each other's business.

Perhaps the strangest and brashest avoidance of the franchise issue was the one pulled off by British author Patricia Wentworth in her series about Miss Maud Silver. Miss Silver, at first glance, is as cozy as a spinster detective can get—white hair, always knitting garments for infants, and so on. She is a retired nanny.

And in her retirement, she has established a thriving business as a Private Enquiry Agent, working out of her antimacassared Victorian parlor. She's already well at it when we meet her. License or no license, it would be a heck of a book to explain just how she pulled this off, and I don't blame Wentworth for never trying to do it.

Another way to flout the franchise is to write about somebody who just doesn't give a damn about it *or* money. A vigilante. The kind of character the late Robert Sampson called the "justice figure."

These characters have it in for somebody special, and so they take it out on anyone in their way.

They might head huge organizations, like the Shadow, or be a part of a small one, like the Four Just Men. Or they might just be loners. The best recent example of this (and the most like a PI, and *certainly* the most hardboiled) is Andrew Vachss's Flood, who visits his wrath on child molesters, as who wouldn't like to?

Everybody else falls somewhere in between.

In real life, for instance, anyone may investigate anything. The Freedom of Information Act doesn't exclude anyone from eligibility. If you get close enough to someone to ask him a question, you have every right in the world to ask it. You can investigate a matter out of personal concern, nagging curiosity or because you feel the need of a hobby.

What you can't do is charge money. At least not legally. Lawrence Block's Matt Scudder sometimes collects something under the table, but he's not supposed to. Also, I suspect this wouldn't fit in with our theoretical callow protagonist.

So now we turn our attention to other sorts of people who get to ask questions for a living.

Journalists are good. In fact, they have it better than PIs in lots of cases. Whereas there are special restrictions on what a PI can do, a reporter gets special privileges, such as not having to reveal his sources. And a reporter can stumble on a major story and be kept there—Woodward and Bernstein were a couple of low-scale city-deskers when they stumbled on Watergate. No reason something like that can't happen to your detective.

And thanks to the First Amendment, you literally can wake

up tomorrow morning and declare yourself a freelance journalist.

Lawyers in this context are even better off. I remember back in the fifties there was a TV series about a lawyer who became a private eye. He must have been nuts. Not only is the lawyer protected from telling the cops what he's learned in defense of his client, he's absolutely forbidden to, except in certain carefully described legal circumstances.

Also, at the proper stage, a lawyer can legally compel people on the other side to answer his questions.

There's no requirement that your attorney ever gets the case into court at all. On the TV show *The Eddie Capra Mysteries*, Capra was a brilliant young lawyer who wanted to get all his cases resolved before they got to court because he hated to wear a tie. Result? A softboiled private eye, and a show that deserved a run much longer than it got.

In his earliest years, the greatest courthouse brain in the history of the genre, Perry Mason, had more than a couple of cases that didn't wind up in the courthouse. Mason in those days was described as a "thinker *and* a fighter," someone who could "work with infinite patience to jockey an adversary into just the right position, then finish him with one terrific punch." They might as well have been talking about Sam Spade.

Another lawyer who functioned as a PI is Harold Q. Masur's Scott Jordan, who flourished in the forties and fifties.

Of course, one problem with the lawyer-PI solution these days is that with the terrific success of Big Trial novels lately, the writer may risk some serious reader wrath if he keeps a lawyer protagonist out of the courtroom. Worse yet, he could well face indignant editorial intimidation, and never get the thing published at all.

Is that it, then? Have we come to the end of the number of sweeps we can run around the difficulties real life throws up in the path of writing about PIs in certain circumstances?

Of course not. Those of us who would please the dedicated PI reader have to be more resourceful than that, just to keep up with the tradition of the genre.

. . . AND CARRY A BIG SCHTICK!

If, as we've shown, the question is *franchise* and franchise is the excuse to become involved in this particular investigation, a seemingly foolproof idea is to tiptoe around the whole issue— to make the matter of Franchise irrelevant in any particular case. And if you can do it once, you can do it a thousand times.

How? By justifying each case on the basis of its already being the detective's business. There's no worry about earning a special fee—what our protagonist is seeking to protect is his or her regular paycheck.

You use what I call a schtick detective.

This is based on my conviction that the deep inner workings of practically any business or profession have their own fascination, secrets and conflicts that can lead to all sorts of crime. Any number of traditional client types may need help in this sort of situation, as does the business itself, and our trouble-shooter.

Instant franchise. Plus instant access to the police, since they'll probably want our protagonist as a witness, and of course as the series rolls along they'll get to know each other better.

Note: I'm postulating a series here because that's what most aspiring authors in the field (most emphatically including me, back in my aspiring days) aspire to write. Needless to say, the "schtick detective" concept can work as well or better on a one-shot, since freshness will also be guaranteed.

Interestingly, most of the examples of schtick detectives come from the cozy end of the mystery spectrum. That clears the deck for more hardboiled practitioners to take advantage of the technique. Lawrence Block's Matt Scudder isn't really being a schtick detective; he's simply risking arrest when he takes some money for a case.

It will be instructive to look at what is being published, in any case, to give you a hint of the kind of schtick you might want to try.

The first modern schtick detective was John Putnam Thatcher, a top executive for the Sloan Guaranty Trust in New

York, created by the writing team known as Emma Lathen. Now, a top vice-president of the third-largest bank in the world may be a bit patrician an image for a PI, but that position carries enormous advantages with it.

Banks are, as Willie Sutton put it, where the money is, and money, murder and mystery have always gone together. In addition, no kind of business gets under way without the assistance and/or meddling of a bank.

This gives the series incredible scope, enabling it to deal with everything from currency fraud to the fried chicken industry without ever suffering a glitch in the Franchise.

The Lathen writing team later created Congressman Benton Safford (D. Ohio), who functions much the same way, though sometimes stretching credulity with his honesty and devotion.

Now, Dick Francis would have already established himself firmly in the PI genre simply on the basis of his books about steeplechase jockey-turned-PI Sid Halley. But he has emerged as one of the top hardboiled writers of the century largely on the basis of the kinds of schtick detectives who can be found around British racing, everything from wine merchants to horse-portrait painters. I don't know for sure what the requirements for a PI license are in the UK, but I feel confident myself that no reader on either side of the Atlantic has been disappointed if a Francis character didn't have one.

The list goes on. Nancy Pickard's Jenny Cain runs a family charity. There are dog breeders and car fanciers.

My own Matt Cobb is a troubleshooter for a TV network and the conglomerate that sustains it. This has taken me a decent number of rungs down the class ladder from John Putnam Thatcher, but it preserves for me the scope of a *really big business*.

In the end, I don't think it really matters. What makes me think of Matt Cobb as a PI is his attitude and his approach. The same thing, I suppose, that led millions of readers to think of John D. MacDonald as the creator of one of the greatest ever fictional private eyes, even though the character never had a license or got close to getting one. Travis McGee simply brazened it out by calling himself a "salvage expert." After all, looking for lost goods is as good a way as any to get involved in a murder plot.

The private eye sensibility, serious or funny, is a shared state of mind between reader and writer. This chapter has been about alternative ways to plausibly take that first step.

After that, talent and enthusiasm should take over.

Senses and Sensibilities

Female PIs in the Nineties

Catherine Dain

During the years when my desk faced a wall, instead of a window as it does now, I had a cork board at eye level where I could tack notes, cartoons, quotations and anything else that struck me as at least momentarily inspirational. The arrangement was random, subject to the whim of the morning. Few thoughts remained tacked to the wall for long.

One of my favorites, one I have kept on the original three-by-five card with a tack hole through it, is from an essay by Natalie Shainess on Antigone, heroine of a Greek tragedy. The daughter of Oedipus, Antigone accepted a death sentence from her uncle Creon rather than agree to a blasphemous but politically expedient act.

"Antigone is not the average woman," Shainess wrote. "But she is what the average woman might become: a person of autonomy, high principle, not narcissistically self-involved, and not defensively suffering, but willing to take risks to live authentically."

I can't come up with a better description of a contemporary female private eye than the one Shainess has given a character from the 2,500-year-old Greek myth.

I wanted to start with that thought because more attention has been given to the female PI's debt of character to her male counterpart than to her place as a direct descendant in a long line of heroic fictional women.

ALL IN THE FAMILY

The family resemblance between male and female PIs is real, of course. The private eye is one of the two distinctly American heroic archetypes (the other is the cowboy), and the only one that could easily accommodate a gender switch when twentieth-century American women began to break out of traditional roles. Or when, as Gloria Steinem put it, we became the men we wanted to marry.

The male private eyes we read about and admired were fearless loners, without friends or family. The Continental Op didn't even have a name. But each of them had a code of honor, a commitment to seeing justice done.

The female PIs kept the fearlessness, the code of honor and the basic idea of autonomy. But autonomy didn't necessarily mean disconnection and alienation, the way it did for the men. As often as not, these women have risked their fictional lives not for strangers, because they have nothing to lose, but for friends, because they care.

And this has been true virtually from the beginning, in 1977. Marcia Muller's Sharon McCone is considered the first of the modern female private eyes. The name of Sharon McCone's agency—All Souls—is a clue that things are different. Maxine O'Callaghan's first Delilah West novel was published in 1980. In that book, *Death Is Forever*, Delilah solves the murder of her husband.

So for female private eyes, autonomy isn't quite the given that it is for men. Instead, it is a quality of character to be carefully protected. And through the tension between autonomy and connectedness, the female private eyes of the nineties are beginning to explore the question: What happens to the story of the hero's journey when the warrior taking the trip is a woman?

HEROINE WITH A THOUSAND FACES

According to Joseph Campbell, the myth of the hero's journey occurs in some form in every culture. There are echoes of this myth in every quest plot, every story of a search for a Holy Grail. But the young warrior enduring the perils of the adventure is almost invariably male.

In this culture, however, in the last fifteen years, as women have become police officers and firefighters and attorneys general in life, fictional women warriors in great numbers have been taking the trip—in the form of female private eyes. The new PIs call forth echoes of classical figures such as Antigone, who gave her life rather than allow her brother's corpse to be desecrated, or the Sumerian goddess Inana, who went to the depths of hell to rescue her lost lover.

So what does this mean to someone who wants to write her own private eye series? It means that in the best series fiction, the central character is slightly larger than life—not the average woman, but what the average woman might become—facing ethical dilemmas and physical danger with equal courage, and developing wisdom through the course of the books.

Do I think reading Greek myths before you start is necessary? No, but I think it helps. One of the truisms of writing is that you write what you read. Thus, all creative writing teachers urge beginning writers to read good books. Walter Van Tilburg Clark, who wrote *The Ox-Bow Incident*, urged students to read a thousand words for every one they wrote. Clark only wrote three novels, though, and I'm sure Charles Dickens would have argued with him.

I read more when I wrote less. Other writers can do both at the same time, a talent I admire.

You can learn from reading bad books, too. But reading good books gives a writer something to strive for. So read mysteries, good and bad, to get a sense of what is going on. You're surely a fan, or you wouldn't be contemplating writing your own. Thus you've read Sara Paretsky and Sue Grafton and Marcia Muller, and probably some of the lesser known figures. (Maybe even Catherine Dain.) But you should also read fiction that has lasted across time and culture to get depth and breadth and bring something new to your character.

You may or may not have read something by Amanda Cross, who writes the Kate Fansler series. If you like hardboiled private eyes, this won't be your taste. But if you haven't read *Writing a Woman's Life*, the book written by Amanda Cross's alter ego, Carolyn Heilbrun, run right out and get it. Now. You will receive valuable insight into the character of the nontraditional woman.

You will also learn why we have tended to view the quest plot as male territory and the romance plot as female. Heilbrun explains that young men have been encouraged to see themselves as the centers of their own story, as striving and ambitious, while young women have been encouraged to see themselves as the princesses waiting to be rescued by the Other, who is the true heroic center of the tale. She argues persuasively for more women to take the quest, as writers and their fictional protagonists.

HEAR HER ROAR

But you do want to start with character, not plot. Writers tell the same stories over and over, whether framed as quest or romance. Erle Stanley Gardner said that he never worried about plot because all his plots were the same—A murders B and C gets blamed for it. I've used that plot a couple of times, too, and I'll probably use it again. Readers knew they weren't going to get any surprises in Gardner's books. But they kept coming back for a beloved character, Perry Mason.

As you think about your own character, remember that you'll have to live with her for a long time if the series is a hit. Many writers start with an idealized version of themselves. I didn't do that because I couldn't see my real self—and certainly not an idealized self—dealing with the kind of physical danger I had put Freddie O'Neal in. So for Freddie O'Neal, I started with something close to what I would want my daughter to be. It was easier to imagine a fearless daughter figure than a fearless ideal self.

Fearlessness is important. Female private eyes have to be even braver than their male counterparts. A number of male private eyes have what Dick Lochte has called a "sociopathic stooge" for a sidekick, someone to call on for extra muscle with no ethical questions asked when the going gets tough and the odds are bad.

But if *she* asks for muscular help, a reader may wince. In the first of the Freddie O'Neal books, *Lay It on the Line*, I thought it was enough that Freddie had the wits to make a telephone call for assistance without her captors realizing that was in fact what she was doing. A fan told me how disappointed she was that Freddie was helped out by a man—and that was even though the man was an aging African-American security guard, far from the traditional knight in shining armor. I've had her ask for help since then—balancing her autonomy with connectedness—but I'm always careful to make certain her competence isn't in question.

So your female private eye must be capable of handling danger by herself. And she will be in danger—your editor will surely insist on it. Or at least mine has. And other women writers have said that their editors have taken the same stance. Antigone must still be threatened by the tomb for taking on the forces of evil. Only now she has to fight her way out to come back in the next book.

WHAT ABOUT LOVE

When you add fearlessness to autonomy, doesn't it become all the harder for her to have any kind of romantic attachment? Certainly. I think that's why so many female sleuths become involved with cops. There are advantages to the idea. The PI has access to police information that way, for one thing. For another, the police officer has a nonromantic reason to be there. No extraneous subplots necessary to deal with the relationship.

But the most interesting advantage has to do with a built-in tension between them. Here is a man who wants to save her from trouble—whose job it is to save people from trouble—and she has to maintain identity and autonomy and competence against that pressure. It saves the author from worrying about a happily-ever-after book in which he becomes the center of her world, otherwise known as the romance plot.

Janet Dawson makes it clear in the Jeri Howard series that the cop and the PI can't live happily ever after. Jeri's ex-husband is a cop.

I've gone in a different direction with Freddie O'Neal's romantic attachments, but that has to do with my personal interest in reversing gender roles in the hero's story. As I mentioned earlier, the goddess Inana went through hell searching for her lost lover. This is a traditional heroic theme—Orpheus and Eurydice are only the most famous pair.

In *Lament for a Dead Cowboy*, Freddie O'Neal had to go through hell to save a lover falsely accused of murder. I used an Elko, Nevada, jail cell in a blizzard as my version of hell. An interesting thing happens when she finds a way to free him, however. He can't quite throw himself into her arms as they ride away into the sunset.

That left her free in the next book to become involved with a university professor who isn't stuck with traditional conceptions of gender roles in relationships. The mythic counterpart to that is the hero's dalliance with a nymph—Odysseus and Calypso, for example. (If a university professor who is open to nontraditional romantic relationship isn't your idea of a nymph, don't write to tell me. Write your own book.)

I didn't expect the relationship to last through a second book. It almost survived a third.

Other PI writers handle the tension between autonomy and connectedness in various ways. I mentioned that Delilah West started out as a grieving widow who had to solve her husband's murder in 1980. Half a dozen books and a decade or so later, Delilah has recovered. But her romantic attachment to a real estate developer whose values are very different from her own assures the reader that Delilah isn't likely to remarry.

Of course, there's no law against a married PI. Some classical male heroes were married (Odysseus, again), a very few male private eyes have been as well (just last year Earl Emerson's PI was added to their ranks), and a number of contemporary female amateur sleuths have sworn to love, honor and cherish, if not obey. Nancy Pickard, Anne Perry, and Sharan Newman have all negotiated that curve successfully with heroines Jenny Cain, Charlotte Pitt and Catherine LeVendeur.

Nevertheless, I think Nancy Drew will grow up and marry Ned Nickerson before Kinsey Millhone or V.I. Warshawski seriously contemplates marriage. For women, even more than for men, there is still a sense that marriage is the end of the adventure and the beginning of the second shift. We've seen that too often in the romance plot. Thus, I can guarantee you that Freddie O'Neal will never be worrying about getting home in time to cook dinner.

A reviewer of *Lament for a Dead Cowboy* commented that the mystery was more important than the relationship. That's true of any novel descended from the quest plot. With a married PI, the romance plot would be tugging at your ear for equal time. Unless you have Nick and Nora Charles as your model (and if you think that's a good idea, reread *The Thin Man* before you start—he was the professional in the family, and they both drank too much), some kind of commitment to single living is the way to go.

CRACKING THE CODE

That brings us to the code of honor. Just as with autonomy and fearlessness, I think this is even more important for a female PI in the nineties than for a male. While there is a certain ends-justifies-the-means ethic in much private eye fiction, I wouldn't try to take it beyond breaking into the villain's apartment and opening his mail, or tinkering with her computer files.

Again, this probably reflects a personal bias. Nevertheless, if your female private eye kills somebody, even justifiably, I believe that as a person of high principle, she ought to deal with the consequences. One of these days we're probably going to see a female PI with a sociopathic stooge—even a female sociopathic PI—but I'm not enthralled with the idea of a female antihero.

Check out *Mallory's Oracle* by Carol O'Connell for the closest thing to a "good" female sociopath currently in print and decide for yourself.

THE REST IS UP TO YOU

Beyond those three qualities—autonomy, bravery and integrity—you're free to make whatever choices appeal to you. Cats or no cats springs immediately to mind. I write that lightheartedly, but it isn't a trivial decision. If you have a cat, you have to use her. Linda Barnes tells of receiving a phone call from her editor asking if Carlotta Carlyle's cat had died. Barnes had simply forgotten to include the cat in the story.

I've heard arguments at recent mystery conferences that a new PI trying to get attention needs to have some sort of gimmick. A gimmick may help—the female PI first novel receiving the most attention as I write this stars Martha Lawrence's Elizabeth Chase, who is psychic—but it won't eliminate the need for a strong, likeable character in a well-told story. And Lawrence delivers these, too.

As for the story . . . the story is what you have when you add character to plot. Story is more than plot. Plot is A murders B and C gets blamed for it. Story is how your own very special detective figures out what happened.

Writing one novel-length story about your character requires commitment and writing an entire series requires compulsion. There must be stories about the character that you need to write.

But that's a subject for another essay.

The Trans-Gender Writer

Finding Your Voice

Wendi Lee

I confess—I'm a trans-gender writer. What the heck is that, you ask? It sounds kind of kinky, doesn't it? OK, I admit it—I made up the word. But it does have a meaning—not as off-center as you might think. No, I don't sit around wearing a fake mustache and chomping on a cigar, an image you might have conjured up in your mind. My definition for a trans-gender writer is a woman who writes from a male point of view, or a man who writes from a female point of view. So you see? It's not what you thought, is it?

We were taught to write what we know. And most writers do, using the voices they know best—male writers feature a male character in their plots, and female writers use the female character. Of course, there have always been exceptions. But these days in the field of PI fiction, more and more women writers are writing series featuring male PI characters. But the opposite is true of female PI fiction—that field is still dominated by women writers.

My first book was from a man's point of view. If you're going to write a novel featuring a private investigator, you might want to consider making your PI of the opposite sex.

WRITING LIKE A GIRL

I began my excursion into the world of trans-gender writing with *Rogue's Gold*, a traditional western novel featuring private investigator Jefferson Birch. My first draft was read by my husband. When he finally put it down, I asked him what he thought. "You write like a girl," he said.

I thought about that for a minute, then I didn't speak to him for about an hour. When I finally calmed down I asked him what he meant.

"Birch doesn't sound like a man. He sounds like a woman disguised as a man.

"Oh," was my response.

In our quest for more equality between men and women these days, writers can sometimes deny or lose sight of their characters' masculine and feminine qualities. So I started to dissect the difference between male and female characters. I came up with five devices that can make your PI character more male or female: character, action, reaction, dialogue and internal dialogue.

In order to get my point across, I'll be treading on some dangerous territory: what defines masculine and feminine. We like to think that in this world, we are created equal, but the truth of the matter is that we all have masculine and feminine traits. What makes a character one gender or the other is a blend of these qualities.

A male character can have feminine qualities just as a female character can have masculine qualities. I think it's particularly difficult to balance these traits, and the temptation for most writers is to create a female character who's a man in disguise or vice versa.

How do we display these masculine and feminine qualities? It's a combination of the way we talk, the way we act, how we react and how we think. For instance, being straightforward is considered a masculine quality. Men, in general, tend to be more direct than women. This is not to say that a woman can't have directness as a quality: It's just considered a masculine characteristic.

The way your characters speak is an excellent way to show whether or not they're direct. A female character might say, "I don't feel like having a drink right now." A male character might say, "I don't want a drink right now."

Both characters are telling us the same thing, but the woman is being indirect by telling you how she feels—she doesn't *want* a drink because she doesn't *feel* like having one.

CHARACTER

One of the easiest ways to create a good PI of the opposite sex is to put something in the character that offsets the stereotypical PI. Robert Parker's Spenser is a gourmet cook. S.J. Rozan's Bill Smith is an ex-Navy man who plays classical piano. My Angela Matelli is an ex-Marine with a big, dysfunctional family. So, you say? The stereotypical private eye doesn't cook cordon bleu, might be ex-military, but sure as hell doesn't like classical music and is usually a loner. In each case, there is something a little off center about the private eye, just enough to make him or her interesting to the reader.

ACTION

Men and women can differ in the way they confront a situation that requires immediate action. In Jeremiah Healy's series character, John Cuddy, we have a Harvard-educated Bostonian who becomes a private investigator. In *Swan Dive*, Cuddy deliberately provokes a bullying suspect during his enquiries:

> Marsh started to come out of the shower, slinging his left leg over the tub wall and making a fist with his right hand. Before he could cock it, I took a quick step forward and jabbed with my index finger hard into the little half-moon hollow we all have just above the breast plate.

Cuddy faces his suspect down, turning the tables on Marsh. His immediate action, using his index finger to immobilize his would-be assailant, is reminiscent of something Jim Rockford might have done on *The Rockford Files*.

In another example of how a male character might handle action, in *The Vanishing Smile*, Earl Emerson's Seattle PI

Thomas Black comes home one night to find an assailant on the steps of his porch:

> Instead of continuing up the stairs and getting cornered on the dark porch, I vaulted the wooden railing into my backyard, sprinted several lengths across the soggy grass, pivoted, and squared off with my assailant.

On the other hand, in *The Good Daughter*, my private eye, Angela Matelli, uses a more pragmatic approach. When she's searching her dead client's house for links to his murder, she hears someone else entering the house. Even though she has permission to be there she would rather avoid a confrontation with whoever is downstairs. Instead, she locks the door to the bedroom, and with some difficulty, opens a window just as the man outside the room starts to break the door down:

> . . . a shoulder thudded against the door. I grabbed the book off the nightstand and tossed it out the window, hoping the sound of a book skidding off the roof approximated the sound of a person taking the roof to the tree and escaping. Then I slid under the bed, hidden by a large fringed bedspread.

Not that Angela doesn't ever face her assailants. For the sake of the story, and because I thought it would be a different way to approach an unknown situation, I had her misdirect her assailants and then hide. It's a good thing, too, because from her hiding place Angela discovers that the two men have broken into the house to look for something incriminating. In this way, she learns something valuable for her investigation—and saves herself a few broken ribs in the meantime.

This isn't to say that female PIs run and hide every time there's trouble, but the writer should be wary of trying to overcompensate when writing a female private eye character. It's tempting to write her as invulnerable—a female superhero who soundly pummels her opponents. Just trying to be one of the guys. The problem is that the guys are *getting* beaten up as well. John Cuddy may have come out of his confrontation all right, but his suspect was a bully who was all bark and no bite. On the other hand, Thomas Black is hit several times with a baseball bat, and is shot at during his encounter. He comes away from the experience with a few cuts and bruises, but at least he's still walking.

A good example of a competent female PI is S.J. Rozan's Lydia Chin. In one scene in her first case, *China Trade*, karate-trained Lydia Chin faces her attackers and defends herself ably until "I saw his foot coming. I moved feebly no distance at all. The slamming pain in my side forced a sound from me, a sad-sounding moan."

Lydia loses the rhythm of karate, and is beaten up just as badly as Thomas Black was in *The Vanishing Smile*. All in a day's work for a private eye, male or female.

Lydia Chin is a good example of the female PI in an action scene. She's brave enough to face her opponents, but she's not a superhero. Being beaten up leaves a person vulnerable, even a tough PI, and Lydia starts to cry when she realizes she's lost her gun.

REACTION

A character's reaction is the outward sign of how he or she responds to other characters around him or her.

An excellent example of this difference is, again, in S.J. Rozan's Lydia Chin/Bill Smith series. In *China Trade*, the reader is in Lydia Chin's first person point of view. In the first chapter, Lydia is hired by the museum where her brother works to investigate the robbery of some valuable porcelains. Her first reaction to being asked to investigate a recent robbery is, "A robbery? When? Was anybody hurt? Why didn't you tell me?" The last question is directed at her brother, Tim, who has his own problems dealing with his little sister investigating the robbery.

Chin's first reaction is outward concern for everyone's

safety. She gets down to the business at hand, but we also get a sense of her distress, and the last question, "Why didn't you tell me?" is accusatory. The reader realizes that there is tension between Lydia Chin and her brother, Tim.

In Rozan's second case, *Concourse*, which is told from Bill Smith's first person point of view, Smith is at the wake of a close friend's nephew. His friend, Bobby, tells him that he wants Smith to investigate his nephew's murder:

> From my jacket pocket I took my own surreptitious flask, handed it to him.
>
> "I'm not supposed to," he told me.
>
> "Who is?"
>
> He eased onto an upholstered folding chair. The chairs were set in rows; I swung one around to face him. He pulled on the flask, handed it back.
>
> "It wasn't your fault," I told him, words no one who needs them ever believes.

Bobby then asks how soon Smith can start, and his reaction is, "Just tell me what you want me to do." His concern is unspoken, but given in direct actions. He doesn't ask if he can help, he tells Bobby to give him some direction.

Rozan uses the passing of the flask to give us more reaction time between Bobby and Bill Smith. We get the sense that they are close, have a history, when they share a flask.

Compare the above scene with the rewritten following:

> From the coffee server I poured two cups and handed him one.
>
> "I'm so sorry for your loss." I reached over and touched his shoulder.
>
> "I'm not supposed to," Bobby said, referring to the coffee.
>
> I shrugged. "One cup won't hurt." I cradled the Styrofoam cup of coffee between my palms. "How are you feeling?"

He shifted in his seat. "How do you think I feel? Like it's my fault."

"It's not your fault. What can I do to help?"

"Find out who did it for me."

While the above scene isn't bad, it's softer. There isn't the sense of shared loss with the passing of the flask when we're writing about Styrofoam coffee cups. Which is more effective? For Bill Smith, a tough private eye, the earlier dialogue makes more sense. He's not a touchy-feely sort of character. For another, more feminine character, the latter scene might play just fine.

DIALOGUE

Earlier in this article I mentioned the difference between "want" and "don't feel like." I was once put on the spot during a local television interview. The interviewer asked me what I meant when my husband told me I wrote like a girl. What was the difference between writing for a female character and writing for a male character? Since I only had seconds to answer I said, "Men think. Women feel."

What I was really trying to say was that women tend to be more in touch with their feelings. Men and women sometimes have a difference in their sense of humor.

Bill Pronzini's Nameless detective has an exchange with his fiancee, Kerry, over a tasteless shower present that means more to her than to him—a pink heart-shaped pillow with the motto, "If It Has Tires Or Testicles, You're Going To Have Trouble With It":

"You don't think it's funny?" she said.

"No. What does it mean?"

"Oh, come on. You're a big boy now. You know what tires and testicles are."

"I known what it means," I said. "I just don't see the point."

"The point," she said, "is that it's funny." But she wasn't chuckling any longer; she wasn't even smiling. "It's a funny saying. It's especially funny to women. That's probably why you don't get it, not being a woman and not understanding women worth a hoot. . . ."

The point is that although not all dialogue has to be looked at carefully to determine if a man or a woman is saying it—we do have the English language in common—sometimes you can play with the dialogue a little, show that your character is a woman or a man through the way they interpret something.

INTERNAL DIALOGUE

This is a character's attitude. What does a woman think about carrying weapons? Lydia Chin cried in frustration at losing her gun. Angela Matelli, on the other hand, is more pragmatic about guns, primarily because she was in the Marines.

I'd been working in my office until ten o'clock. Just before I left I tugged open the bottom left-hand drawer. I drew out my Star to carry with me as I walked to the T in the dark. Just in case.

Still, in a careless moment, Angela sticks the gun in her bag. She's attacked on a small, dark street and can't get to her gun. Her internal dialogue reflects her thoughts as she turns the tables on her attacker.

I considered shooting at him but immediately dismissed it. The shots might go wild and injure an innocent bystander at the end of the alleyway, or shooting him might antagonize the mugger enough that he would take someone else hostage.

Bill Smith in *Concourse* gets into trouble on behalf of a stranger who's being beaten up. After entering the fray, Smith gets hit a few times and decides he's had enough:

> Before the next kick I fumbled into my jacket, swept
> out my .38.
> "Freeze!"
> His eyes met mine for the briefest second; I went cold
> when I saw what was in them. . . .

Smith doesn't run through the results of using his weapon;
he just knows he needs it. But the consequences run through
Angie's mind as she trains her gun on her attacker.

Another view comes from Marcia Muller's Sharon McCone
in *Till the Butchers Cut Him Down*:

> In spite of the fact that I'm an excellent shot and enjoy
> practicing on the range with my .38, I try to avoid carrying
> it unless it's absolutely necessary.

This internal dialogue shows McCone to be a cautious person, a good trait to have in the business of private investigation.

But there is the internal dialogue of emotions. Women will
analyze their emotions, sometimes on a play-by-play basis. So
it isn't out of the realm of possibility for your female PI to think
about her relationship with someone, or to flash back to an
unpleasant time and relive it. A male character might flash back
briefly, but will push any unpleasantness from his mind and
concentrate on the here and now.

One of the best writers of the male PI character is D.C.
Brod, whose character Quint McCauley is introspective about
his relationship with former girlfriend Elaine:

> I jabbed my cigarette into the ashtray, using the move-
> ment to avert my eyes. She reads me too well. But at that
> point there was no way I could come right out and say: It
> feels like we're breaking up here, and I don't know how or
> even if we should stop it.

The character examines his feeling, admitting to guilt, stupidity and being ungrateful, but the internal dialogue doesn't come across as soft—maybe a bit vulnerable, but that's all right in a male character. Not all male PIs should be inaccessible. Quint shows that it's possible for a male character to talk about feelings without sounding too sappy.

AND FINALLY

The experience of trans-gender writing has given me a new appreciation for men and the way they think and act. One of the things I've tried to stress in this article is the fact that you shouldn't be afraid to try your hand at writing a character of the opposite sex. If your male character isn't working for you, change his sex and see what happens. Maybe he's just a woman in disguise.

SETTING

A Trip Into the Hinterlands

Jan Grape

What is the definition of a regional book or story? Any book or story *not* set in New York or Los Angeles? Private eye stories set in Galveston or Cincinnati or Albuquerque or Cape Cod or Cedar Rapids or Austin would qualify. The mean streets of Chicago and San Francisco probably would not be considered regionals to most readers, reviewers, editors and booksellers. Yet in the hands of the many skillful private eye writers of today, a story in which any setting becomes somewhat like a minor character has the feel of a regional even if the setting is in New York or Los Angeles.

Think about this definition: Any author whose story takes you where you've never been before—even if it's familiar territory—and where that author's creativity lets you smell, hear, see and feel an area like never before is a regional.

Maybe a regional is any setting an editor who is publishing your book says is a regional.

Is writing a regional private eye any different? Not really. A good story is a good story no matter the setting, but judge for yourselves with these prime examples.

The Yellowstone River is a great gray ribbon of water that is born high in the mountains near Yellowstone Park, nurtured each year by the melt of alpine snowpacks. At Billings it gradually drifts to the northeast where it eventually joins the great Missouri just inside the North Dakota border. Grizzlies, as big as houses, roamed here once as did mastodons and primitive peoples veering off the Great

North Trail. Buffalo herds were so vast, some say it took weeks for an entire herd to pass one point, so powerful they could knock a train off its track if they were stampeding.

EXCERPT FROM *THE KILLING OF MONDAY BROWN*, BY SANDRA WEST PROWELL, FEATURING PHOEBE SIEGEL.

The ocean roared and pushed him close to shore. Carver felt the equilibrium lent by deep water desert him. His toes and palms scraped on the grit and broken shells of sea-tossed sand. Breakers curled and flattened out, then frothed around his suddenly heavy and awkward body, which belonged to land. Dragging his bad leg, he crawled through shallow water toward the beach.

As he emerged from the water, the fierce Florida sun bore down on him.

EXERPT FROM *BLOODFIRE*, BY JOHN LUTZ, FEATURING FRED CARVER.

The night air was thick and damp as I drove South along Lake Michigan. I could smell rotting alewives like a faint perfume on the heavy air. Little fires shone here and there from late-night barbecues in the park. On the water a host of green and red running lights showed people seeking relief from the sultry air. On shore traffic was heavy, the city moving restlessly, trying to breathe. It was July in Chicago.

I got off Lake Shore Drive on Randolph Street and swung down Wabash under the iron arches of the elevated tracks. At Monroe I stopped the car and got out.

EXCERPT FROM *INDEMNITY ONLY*, BY SARA PARETSKY, FEATURING V.I. WARSHAWSKI.

All right, I'll tell you. But you have to promise not to laugh, okay? I'm a private investigator. In Nashville, Tennessee.

Stop snickering.

No, I do not wear a trench coat, or a double-breasted suit, or a homburg. I don't smoke cigarettes or drink straight Scotch out of the desk drawer in my office, and I don't smack women around.

These days they hit back. Hard.

Neither do I sing country music, nor write country music, nor even listen to country music. My tastes run to jazz, and I did not just fall off the turnip truck. I was born here, but I went to school in Boston, spent my junior year abroad in France, and wear shoes almost every day. I can lay on a country accent as thick as molasses on a frosty morning, if I have to. But I also throw in enough Newport, Rhode Island, to make Tom Wicker sound like a hick.

EXCERPT FROM *DEAD FOLKS BLUES* BY STEVEN WOMACK, FEATURING HARRY JAMES DENTON.

What do these openings have in common? They evoke a visual picture in your mind of a place, a location with the strongest sense of immediacy. You could have hopped on a transporter pad, said "Beam me up, Scotty" and landed in Billings, Montana, or on the Florida Coast or in Chicago, Illinois or in Nashville Tennessee.

This is a big part of the magic of reading a regional private eye story—you are there. In that particular location and in no other place would that character be right for that particular story.

And why is that important? Who knows? Maybe it's a different reason for each of us. For instance, the wonderment of vicariously visiting a place where a reader has never been or even if they had been there they would have never seen the place with the same eyes as the author does.

A writer friend recently mentioned talking to a bookstore owner and the bookstore person said, "I never read books set in Dallas. Reading about Texas doesn't appeal to me at all."

My writer friend asked, "So what is the setting of the books you like to read?"

"New York," came the reply. "Maybe Chicago. That's it."

My friend told me he was stupefied for an answer. Then he told me, "I couldn't believe it. Look at all the wonderful reading this person is missing out on."

How would you like knowing a bookstore owner is limiting himself like that? Hope this attitude doesn't carry over to his book buying, don't you?

To learn of another city or town or state besides where that reader actually lives can be most fascinating. Readers enjoy reading about places they are planning to visit while on vacation or places they'd like to go to for a vacation.

People also like reading about where they currently live or once lived. They like reading about the main character driving down a particular street and thinking, "I recognize this. I know where that private eye is headed. I've been there." For many readers, that's part of the fun of reading about their hometown is driving the same streets as a character (or the author) does.

Those tiny brushstrokes the author uses to give a visual picture of that specific location often gives the reader a totally new perspective on that town or area. Even if that reader spent days or weeks visiting, those tiny nuances give that reader new insights.

Come along on a reading journey and you'll see what diverse locations and settings exist.

San Quentin Prison stands on a windswept headland on San Francisco Bay. At first sight it does not look like such a bad place: its sandstone-colored walls and red roof are architecturally imposing. The cypress-fringed hall that abuts them and a row of sturdy palms along the shoreline lend the natural setting a certain charm. The waters of the bay are azure or green or steel gray, depending on the weather, dotted with sailboats and the sleek ferries that ply their way from Marin County's Larkspur Landing to San Francisco. Not such a bad place at all.

But as you approach the prison's iron gates down a

narrow lane lined mostly with ramshackle houses, you hear the rumble of loudspeakers in the yard and the monotonous hum of the generators that keep the huge physical plant functioning. You see the guard tower and the floodlights and warning signs, and the weary hopelessness on the eyes of the people who trickle through the visitor's entrance. The wind feels colder: It carries the stench of stagnant water and an indefinable decay.

EXCERPT FROM *THE SHAPE OF DREAD* BY MARCIA MULLER, FEATURING SHARON MCCONE.

How many prison books have been written? Tens, dozens, hundreds? How many movies with San Quentin? But has anyone ever transported you there more vividly than Muller has?

Or come walk along these mean streets to a place you've probably never been before.

When they speak about Cleveland's big comeback, from the edge of insolvency, from being a favorite target of stand-up comedians, it is most often to the Flats that people point, and with every justification. It had been the warehouse district in the early part of the century, situated as it is on a low-lying shelf of land dividing downtown Cleveland from the waters of the Cuyahoga River. After the river traffic slowed down and moved elsewhere most of the warehouses were abandoned to rot, rust and rats. Then just a few years ago some enterprising folk decided to buy up the warehouses, gut and renovate them, and make the Flats *the* trendy place to go and see and be seen in the city. Suddenly the ghostly old warehouses were transformed into the most elegant and pricey restaurants and glittering night spots in northern Ohio, and it was a rare night indeed that the Flats was not jammed with upscale cars and fashionably dressed people of all ages, there for a great meal, a good time, or to meet each other and connect. Places never before heard of, like Danny's,

Sammy's, DiPoo's, the River Rat, and the Watershed, were turning customers away on weekend nights and, during the warm weather even midweek was holiday time in the Flats. I didn't hang around down there very much, as I rarely had anyone to take to dinner and discos were just not my style.

EXCERPT FROM *PEPPER PIKE*, BY LES ROBERTS, FEATURING MILAN JACOVICH.

Can't you see and smell and taste and hear the Flats of Cleveland? Don't those words make you want to pack bags and head to Cleveland for a visit? But maybe in late spring before that wind gets too cold and malevolent.

Or a reader might enjoy picking up this little known fact— well, perhaps it's not little known to millions of people in the area, but the remainder of Americans probably don't know this:

Windsor, Ontario, sits directly across the river from Detroit. Thanks to a kink in the Detroit River, Windsor is actually south of Detroit—the only place where any part of Canada is south of any part of the United States. Ben Perkins, student of geography, they call me.

Many Detroiters tend to regard Windsor as a suburb of Detroit. They think of Windsor as a less-favored cousin, maybe an aspirant to U.S. citizenship. I suppose that's because it's so damned easy to get over there thanks, since 1929, to the Ambassador Bridge and the Detroit-Windsor tunnel, plus liberal border crossing policies employed by both sides.

EXCERPT FROM *THE BACK DOOR MAN*, BY ROB KANTNER, FEATURING BEN PERKINS.

That small geography lesson lends an air of authenticity to the story and adds another dimension to the character. No other character might think in that way about the cities of Windsor and Detroit. That particular character knows his city and is happy to tell you about it.

Or how about small town U.S.A.? A place you might not dream of being big enough to have a private eye, but it does have one. Just one PI—and wait until you meet this guy:

> I might as well admit it. I'm not exactly in the best of shape. I used to be, back when I was in Louisville, back when I was still a cop. The possibility of somebody shooting your ass if you're a step slow is a real powerful motivator. Back then I worked out in the gym three or four days a week. And I ran two miles a day on an indoor track.
>
> Here in Pigeon Fork (population 1,511), I reckon I just don't have the same kind of motivation. I also don't have a gym or an indoor track any more and the idea of running down the gravel road I live on doesn't exactly appeal to me. Somehow, I don't think I'd particularly enjoy running with rocks in my shoes. Or with my neighbors coming out on their porches wondering what's chasing me.
>
> EXCERPT FROM *RUFFLED FEATHERS*, BY TAYLOR MCCAFFERTY, FEATURING HASKELL BLEVINS.

You become so intrigued in reading the story you often don't even notice how the city has become a secondary character. It would be almost impossible to read about Bill Pronzini's Nameless detective in a setting other than San Francisco. San Francisco is so much a part of Nameless and his life. Those different parts make up the sum of who Nameless is and why he is like he is and how he understands human nature by knowing his city and its citizens: the old grandfather Italian neighborhoods, the trollies, Chinatown, Fisherman's Wharf and the marina and the foggy nights.

Look how the mood the author creates fits the character and in turn the situation:

> The tourists were out in droves despite the weather; there were more white faces along Grant than there were

Chinese. The street, Chinatown's main thoroughfare, had undergone a cosmetic facelift in recent years. Everywhere you looked there was what the younger generation of Chinese referred to derisively as "pigtail architecture," pagoda style building facades, street lamps, even public telephone booths designed to give the tourist an "asthetic" Chinese atmosphere. . . . Grant Avenue wasn't the real Chinatown; it was glitter and sham, a Disneyland version of Hong Kong or Canton, a visitor's enclave of souvenir shops, Chinese art and jade merchants, fancy restaurants, dark little bars. The real Chinatown was along Stockton and Kearny Streets, in the back alleys and narrow streets on both sides of Grant. That was where you found the bundle shops, where seamstresses worked fourteen-hour days at their sewing machines for starvation wages; the tenements and projects; the social clubs and gambling parlors, and dingy Chinese theaters; the joss houses, the herb shops, the exotic groceries, the Chinese-language newspapers; the Chung Fat Sausage Company and the Golden Gate Fortune Cookie Factory; and the First Chinese Baptist Church and the Chinese Cemetery Association and the ironically named Hang On Realty and Insurance. That was where you found the poverty, attitudes, and a way of life that had changed remarkably little in over a century.

EXCERPT FROM *DRAGONFIRE*, BY BILL PRONZINI, FEATURING NAMELESS.

Historical facts can also bring a setting to life:

"Just for the hell of it we ran Blum's prints. We got a positive."

"He told me he'd never been printed."

"He must've forgot," Alderdyce said. "We didn't mess with the FBI. They destroy their records once a subject turns seventy. We got a match in a box of stuff on its way to the incinerator because it was too old to bother feeding into the computer. There is no Leonard Blum. But Leo Goldblum got to know these halls during prohibition, whenever the old rackets squad found it prudent to round up the Purple Gang and ask questions."

"Blum was a Purple?"

"Nice kids, those. When they weren't gunning each other down and commuting to Chicago they found time to ship bootleg hootch across the river from Canada. That was Goldblum's specialty. He was arrested twice for transporting liquor from the Encore docks and drew a year's probation in 'twenty-nine on a Sullivan rap. Had a revolver in his pocket."

"That explains why he never registered his guns," I said. Licenses aren't issued to convicted felons. "That was a long time ago, John."

"Yeah, well, there's something else. Ever hear of Bloody July?"

"Sounds like the name of a punk rock group. No, wasn't that when they killed Jerry Buckley?"

<small>EXCERPT FROM "BLOODY JULY," A SHORT STORY BY LOREN D. ESTLEMAN IN THE *GENERAL MURDERS* ANTHOLOGY, FEATURING AMOS WALKER.</small>

Sometimes you can show two sides of a city: one familiar to the reader and one not. Take these two views of Brooklyn, for example:

My father lived on Ovington Avenue, which was also Sixty-eighth Street, between Fourteenth and Fifteenth Avenues. Some people call this section Bensonhurst but on the map it says Borough Park. His house—the house I'd grown up in—is a one-family wood frame, semiattached on one side. The shingles were the same ugly green they'd been when I was a kid. The houses on the block were basically the same, with a two- or three-family brick thrown in every so often, like cavities. Like so many south Brooklyn blocks, this one was packed with homes, at least fifty-five of them.

I started to feel hemmed in as soon as Sam turned her car into the block. I felt like I had more room to breathe in an apartment on a block of brownstones than on a block like this.

EXCERPT FROM *NO EXIT FROM BROOKLYN*, BY ROBERT J. RANDISI, FEATURING NICK DELVECCHIO.

A familiar image of Brooklyn, one most readers expect. But what about another section of Brooklyn? New and different images, maybe? An entirely different city from what you may have thought—same book, same author:

Sheepshead Bay was a whole different Brooklyn, all the way at the southern tip. It was old homes, small wood-frame houses that used to be summer homes but were now year-round. A lot of them stood below sidewalk level now because they had been built before there was a sidewalk.

The main drag of Sheepshead Bay was Emmons Avenue which was right on the bay. On one side were the docks, and if you got there later in the day, the boats were all in with their catches, selling fresh fish. The other side was lined with restaurants, most of them seafood places, the best in the city. On week-ends there were flea markets in the parking lots, and the streets on both sides of Emmons were lined with street vendors.

EXCERPT FROM *NO EXIT FROM BROOKLYN*, BY ROBERT J. RANDISI, FEATURING NICK DELVECCHIO.

When you read a Spenser book, don't you see him sculling on the river? And all because of that opening scene in the TV series. Or you see Spenser cooking or jogging. So the idea of how Boston looks is colored more by the twenty-seven-inch screen than we like to admit. Visualize another Boston with another author:

When I drive a cab, I keep strictly away from the Long-wood Medical area, preferring a tricky left turn and a cres-cent-shaped detour onto the Riverway to avoid the whole Hospital Row, which boasts—in addition to Helping Hand— Children's Hospital, Beth Israel Hospital, Brigham and Women's, the Deaconess, the Dana-Farber Cancer Institute, and probably a few healthcare havens that have opened since the last time I checked. The traffic is appall-ing. People late for doctor's appointments, hurrying to give birth, or racing to see loved ones *in extremis* tend to be less than mindful of their turn signals. Add the fact that every intersection in the one-mile stretch has its very own traffic light, and the result is a caliber of gridlock unique even in Boston.

EXCERPT FROM *SNAPSHOT*, BY LINDA BARNES, FEATURING CARLOTTA CARLYLE.

Or search out new facts about a well-known city with the likes of the following:

In a city known for its live shows and touted as the Entertainment Capital of the World, Las Vegas has made some abrupt changes to the contrary. The music for the production shows at the major Strip hotels is now on tape, replacing the live bands with music prerecorded by musi-cians who are now out of work.

The majority of the other hotels that feature star poli-cies—big name singers and comedians—have reduced their house bands to skeleton combos or in some cases eliminated them altogether. The lounges for the most part hire self-contained groups of fewer and fewer musicians. Thanks to synthesizers, drum machines, and the weakening of the musician's union, Top Forty groups dominate the entertainment for audiences that are only killing time be-tween gambling and eating.

The jazz scene is another story. A handful of bars try

jazz for a few weeks or a few months, refuse to advertise or pay decent dough, then blame it on the musicians if it doesn't pan out. The owners quickly move on to something else.

EXCERPT FROM *DEATH OF A TENOR MAN*, BY BILL MOODY, FEATURING EVAN HORNE.

Up the West Coast, Seattle is a city with steep hills and bays and boats and ferries—but how about the traffic?

These days the rush hour was omnipresent. The surrounding suburban territory had filled up at a rate that had exceeded even the most pessimistic long-range plans. Long the butt of local jokes, a series of phantom freeway ramps had for the last twenty-five years surrounded the city. Connecting to the extant highway system, but leading off only into space, they had been built to accommodate the traffic of the future. The future had never come.

By the time the highway department had gotten around to connecting these mystery ramps to the existing road system, the traffic of the future had become the traffic of the past and was now equally horrific in all directions. There were as many people trying to get back into the city at six in the evening as there were people trying to leave. Seemingly overnight, the sticks had become the burbs, and the burbs had filled to the brim.

EXCERPT FROM *WHO IN HELL IS WANDA FUCA?*, BY G.M. FORD, FEATURING LEO WATERMAN.

Moving even more westward to a region often considered foreign country but which in reality is our forty-ninth state:

Creek Street is a row of wood frame houses built on pilings over an estuary. Late in the year the salmon run up the creek to spawn by the thousands. A hundred years ago the street was Ketchikan's red-light district, where miners, sailors, and the curious were offered all manner of sport: booze from Canada, opium courtesy of the Chinese cannery workers, and whores who were mostly women from Scandinavian or Eastern European countries, occasionally a Negress. People say that every third week you could find a man's body floating with the tide out to the bay. It was lucky for everyone that the police didn't ask too many questions. During the red-light era, it was said to be the only body of water where men and salmon went upstream to do the same thing.

The houses are old and weathered and the wooden siding seems damp even if it hasn't rained in days.

EXCERPT FROM *THE CURIOUS EAT THEMSELVES*, BY JOHN STRALEY, FEATURING CECIL YOUNGER.

How delightful to pick up a new private eye book and learn about a new city, state or country. To feel as though you've begun a journey—a trip, a cruise, a vacation—while reading, all snug in your favorite armchair. That was always the enticement, the seduction of reading for me, and it still is. And that's one reason regional PI books remain popular. If you're thinking of writing a private eye book, consider the setting—who else knows your town like you do? Who else can bring out the little known historical, geographic or geological facts? Who else knows the people who live and work right in your own hometown? Your town, U.S.A., may turn out to be the best possible setting for the next intriguing regional private eye story.

Private Eye Witness

Historical PI Fiction

Max Allan Collins

review of one of my Nathan Heller novels, not so long ago, included an observation that went something like this: "Max Allan Collins loves two things—a good private eye yarn, and research." The reviewer went on to rhapsodize about my love of research, perhaps a reaction to the bibliographic author's notes at the conclusion of each of my Nathan Heller novels, chatty essays which have come to be one of the signatures of those books.

I don't love research. Not at all. In fact, right now I'm staring at a Heller deadline that I may well miss because my research is going so slowly. I'm not even sure I love writing. I love *parts* of the writing process; who doesn't love their job when the work is going quickly, smoothly and well? But finding the right word, sentence, paragraph needed to compose yet another page, in what needs to become a chapter if I hope ever to finish the novel in progress, is often agony.

Like most writers, what I really truly love is *having* written—holding a finished manuscript in my hands, particularly one I have read through and found acceptable.

And I feel the same way about research. I love *having* researched. I love sitting down to write with a comfort level reflecting my knowledge that every fact I'm going to need is somewhere within my reach (usually on the library cart that is now a permanent next-door neighbor to my desk).

DON'T TRUST THE WITNESSES

Researching, like writing, does have its joys. I have been a used-book store junkie since early childhood, and there's a great deal of pleasure digging out-of-print volumes from back-of-the-store shelves and basement back-stock storehouses. One of my great research victories of recent years was while I was on my hands and knees in a walk-down Honolulu used bookstore whose knowledgeable manager assured me she had nothing like what I'd requested: an early thirties Hawaii travel guide. Within minutes of being told this, I was holding in my hands a 1930 volume entitled *So You're Going to Hawaii*, which became the Bible of my "Heller Goes to Hawaii" novel, *Damned in Paradise* (1996). Six bucks.

You do have to be sort of a private eye to properly research. You have to distrust witnesses (like the above-mentioned book-store manager) and root out information for yourself. You have to be resourceful and even brave. My longtime research associate and I have, on occasion, lied over the phone to the relatives of gangsters (in disguised efforts to discover whether those gangsters were still living—I don't want to get sued, or shot); been chased by a pack of wild dogs (in Cleveland's infamous Kingsbury Run, researching my Eliot Ness novel *Butcher's Dozen*); and sat around the pool at the Flamingo Hotel in Las Vegas as one of Bugsy Siegel's pit bosses pointed out where the bodies were buried (hint: rose bushes).

As I've indicated, I prefer old-book stores to libraries, but I use both. The problem with library material is that you have to check them out, and for a limited time; photocopying entire books can get expensive, and so can "overdue" fines.

USE INFORMANTS

Because my historical novels are set in the twentieth century, I depend on libraries largely for newspaper research, which is a considerable part of the Heller approach. I like to look at multiple newspapers reporting on the same event whenever possible; the novel in which Heller meets John Dillinger, *True*

Crime (1984), benefited from my going to the trouble of seeing how every paper in Chicago reported the Dillinger shooting— each one had lined up different eyewitnesses, and each one had different cops on the payroll, so I got a much bigger, richer picture that way.

My research assistant, George Hagenauer, is so valuable to me I often refer to him as a collaborator (except when cashing royalty checks). If you are considering writing a series of novels with a historical setting, or a work of considerable length, I would advise seeking out a friend with an interest in that historical period, or a bent toward research (or, if you're very lucky, both). Research assistants are expensive, and while George is paid for his work, he is one of my best friends and treats me fairly and even generously. I can call George up almost any evening and find him not only patient with me, but eager to dig in and discuss the case we're exploring.

As the Hellers have gained a following, I've also found a number of fans eager to do research for nothing more than expenses, credit and the occasional pat on the back. Lynn Myers hits the databases for me, and finds obscure books and magazines on interlibrary loan. I could not have written *Blood and Thunder* (1995) without Louisiana resident Michael Wynne; the book deals with the assassination of Huey Long, a subject dear to Mike's heart. History isn't just events, it's setting, and Mike helped me understand and get a feel for Louisiana in the thirties. George Hagenauer grew up in Chicago (his uncle lived next door to Eliot Ness) and it's thanks to him that Nate's attitudes reflect that town.

GET AN ATTITUDE

Notice I mentioned "attitudes," not just geographic details. Our job as writers is not to just lay in a travel-guide background, however colorful; we must attempt to understand the people and their times—no small task. In fact, every time I set out to write a Nate Heller novel, I have a mild panic attack with some amnesia mixed in. How *do* I do this?

As most writers have discovered, every time you set out to write a novel, the wheel must be reinvented. Even those writers who create a "formula" must struggle to fill in their self-created blanks with imaginative variations on character and plot. (The quotes around "formula" designate my skepticism that there is any such thing as formula writing—every Perry Mason novel, for example, is distinct from the others and yet Erle Stanley Gardner is frequently dismissed as a "formula" writer. By the way, I have been a critic/reviewer, and I have been a novelist, and let me tell you—novelist is harder.) While certain plot devices recur in the Heller novels, I'm proud that each of the books so far is its own book—Heller is the constant, while the stories always go their own quirky way.

DO THE LEGWORK

Let's discuss, briefly, research trips. The best thing about them is they're deductible. The worst thing is that most of the locations you go to will have changed so much that you risk having irrelevant modern images fixed in your head when you need vintage images. Honolulu and Waikiki had changed incredibly since 1932, the time of *Damned in Paradise*; yet pockets of it were the same—the ocean, for instance, is a pretty big pocket as pockets go—so the journey was definitely worthwhile.

The best thing about research at the actual location of your story is hitting the bookstores (especially used-book stores), where you will find local and regional publications that would never turn up in your part of the world.

KNOW YOUR MAN

And now, finally, we have arrived at the private eye. My PI, Nathan Heller, works in Chicago beginning in the early thirties and, at this point (nine novels and eight short stories), has taken a case as late as 1953; it's my intention to move all the way to the mid-sixties before stopping. I'm writing his "memoirs," and he ages and changes with the years; for example, after Heller serves in the Marines on Guadalcanal (*The Million-Dollar*

Wound, 1986), he's a different guy.

Private eyes—or private-eye-like detectives—can exist in any time frame, and research techniques change little if you choose, say, Nero's Rome over Capone's Chicago (you might find fewer newspapers on microfilm for the former, admittedly . . . but better, more detailed scholarship than for the latter).

One of the great challenges for the aspiring private eye writer is to develop not only a detective distinctly your own, but an approach that is yours, as well. "The memoirs of Nate Heller" reflect my longtime love of the private eye story, but my reluctance to write a contemporary PI tale. I felt the private eye was a child of a specific time period—the thirties, forties and fifties, when the three great private eye writers reigned: Dashiell Hammett, Raymond Chandler, Mickey Spillane. Sometime in the 1970s, I was re-reading for the umpteenth time *The Maltese Falcon* (the single greatest private-eye novel) and noticed that the copyright date was 1929.

"Hmmm," I said inside my head. "The year of the St. Valentine's Day Massacre . . . Sam Spade and Al Capone were contemporaries."

In the comic-book trade, we call that a light bulb going off. I immediately realized that instead of having Philip Marlowe meet an Al Capone type (as Chandler from time to time had him do), I could have Al Capone meet a Philip Marlowe type. The PI as a literary device had existed long enough to actually have a historical context.

I was not the first to figure this out. I was having this revelation about the time *Chinatown* appeared (the greatest private eye movie); screenwriter Robert Towne (and a handful of novelists, principally Andrew Bergman and Stuart Kaminsky) had also noticed the PI's historical context.

Kaminsky has been particularly successful with his Toby Peters novels, which have a Hollywood setting. What I do with Nate Heller differs from the Kaminsky/Bergman approach in that they are essentially writing what I would characterize as a "period" PI novel. They skillfully use real people and places of the recent, *noir* part as a backdrop for their tales. But they don't base their stories on real events (conversely, Towne based *Chinatown* loosely on real events, but incorporated no historical figures).

The period PI novel (and, again, by this I refer to that period during which the fictional private eye first flourished, roughly 1927 through 1960) is an established subgenre now. It's a sort of early-twentieth-century western, and if it hasn't quite flourished, such novels continue to find publishers and audiences. And every now and then, there's a period PI TV show or movie.

The private eye is an appealing character in a historical setting for the same reasons PIs work well in contemporary times: They are a window not only on the case at hand, but on the times. Filtering a complex historical landscape through the focal point of a PI makes life easier on both writer and reader. For example, one of the reasons this lifetime resident of Iowa "got away" with writing about Louisiana in the thirties is that my detective was a stranger there, too—he was learning the ways of Huey Long's kingdom even as I was.

My own technique (which I am proud, and irritated, to say is now being imitated) is to center on a true crime, research it as if I were planning to write a nonfiction book on the subject, and then present my thoughts on the case in the form of a classic hardboiled detective novel. Part of my approach is to pick (at least in the novels—I'm looser about this in short stories) a case shrouded in the mists of controversy and history, true unsolved crimes that Nate Heller and I can finally crack.

Another central part of my approach is to use the Chandler-style first person, a tactic I was strongly advised against (I changed literary agents because of it). The Heller novels are long—some of them are very long. *True Detective* was the longest first person private eye novel ever written, until I wrote the Lindbergh novel, *Stolen Away* (1991). The conventional wisdom was (and still is, to some degree) that you "can't" write a first person novel of that length—too daunting for the reader to be locked into that point of view.

I feel the limitation of the single point of view is an important organizing element in my true-crime tours; and I also feel the first person private eye voice at its best is the most distinctively, purely American voice in literature since Huckleberry Finn.

I have carved out a distinct niche for myself with this approach, and if you mimic me, I will be flattered and hate you. You will also, most likely, be zinged for imitating me, if a knowledgeable reviewer lays hands on your book.

But if you "love research and a good private eye yarn," develop your own approach, your own brand of character, choose your own time frame, and bring it all to life. The biggest pitfall *is* falling in love with research—that or hating research so much that you feel compelled to include every scrap of it you dug out.

The most important part of the word "history" is the last five letters. If you let the research tail wag the narrative dog, *you're* history.

Write What You Know and Fake the Rest

The Importance of Knowing What You're Writing About

Jerry Keneally

I do think it is important to know your subject; however, there are times when you can know it too well, and bore the reader. There is a fine line between keeping the reader interested and weighing him or her down with information that may seem fascinating to you, but pulls *them* away from the story. That's what fiction writers are, after all—storytellers.

Of course there are writers who, through their talent, can shovel large amounts of techno-data into their work and still keep us on the edge of our reading chairs. Clancy's *Hunt for Red October* is an excellent example. The atomic submarine became a central character in the book and I wanted to know all those intimate little details that Clancy reportedly gleaned from visits to public libraries.

Even those of us without Mr. Clancy's skills find the public library a must. I spend so much time there that I'm known as the oldest latchkey child in the San Mateo Library system.

Research. My biggest problem with research is disciplining myself so that I don't get carried away with the search. More often than not, I end up knowing more about the subject than is necessary for the book I'm working on.

A few years back I had the pleasure of going to London

for Bouchercon, *the* mystery writer's convention. A friend who is a San Francisco policeman put me in contact with two London detectives. One was in charge of the wonderfully named "Murder Squad" and the other was a retired Scotland Yard inspector who was working as chief of security for the Bank of England. Both were very nice chaps who treated me with much more respect than I deserved—trips to Scotland Yard, the Black Museum, a ride on a police boat on the Thames. Nearly all of the places we journeyed to ended up in the Polo book *Special Delivery*.

We got into a discussion of English mystery writers, and the name of P.D. James came up. Now Ms. James is a terrific writer, and her books contain a great deal of very descriptive and very accurate background and forensic materials. According to the two London cops, however, Inspector Adam Dalgliesh is a joke. He'd never last a day in real life.

Granted, a policeman is a tough reviewer for a mystery book, but both of them thought that the Inspector Morse series (the books, not the TV shows) was very believable. Perhaps it's all those pints of ale Morse consumes.

FORENSICS

The present-day mystery writer has to seriously consider the advancements in forensics.

We all got a DNA education during the O.J. Simpson trial. We also learned that the cops and D.A.s still screw up on a regular basis. Bad for them, but helpful to us writers.

In the good old days, the private eye could trudge into a room, peel a pistol from a dead man's hands, wipe it clean with his handkerchief and drop it alongside a potted plant. Or perhaps another dead body. They seemed to stumble over a lot of corpses in those days.

It doesn't quite work that way now. A true case that took place in Florida recently is an interesting example. The bad guy murdered his wife, then went through that routine of taking out his handkerchief and wiping his fingerprints from the murder weapon. The police found the gun. No fingerprints, but there was a mucus smear from the handkerchief. Hello DNA—goodbye bad guy.

There's another new piece of equipment on the market that may have us all writing science fiction in the future. Example: A stubble-faced, grubby-looking gentleman staggers into a posh restaurant. The maitre d' gives him a quick look and is about to signal for the bouncer. But he checks his computer first. "Ah, Mr. Swigglehorn, so good to see you again." He leads Swigglehorn to the best seat in the house and instructs the sommelier to bring the gentleman his usual, a bottle of Dom Perignon, caviar and rack of lamb.

What the maitre d' saw on his computer screen was the results of a thermogram. An infrared camera had scanned Mr. Swigglehorn's face, recognizing it immediately even though when last seen Swigglehorn was well-barbered and clean-shaven. Once the computer recognized the face, all of the information regarding that customer's dining and drinking habits appeared on the screen.

A facial thermogram is more or less a fingerprint of the branching of blood vessels on the face. Like fingerprints, no two people, even identical twins, have the same thermogram.

Beards (real or false), plastic surgery, Tammy-Faye-thick makeup—none of it will fool the infrared camera.

Think of the plots this technology will destroy. No more master spies sneaking on airplanes. No more disguised bank robbers or jewel thieves.

There is even a DNA pen, wherein the subject's DNA is bonded to the ink. Widely forged celebrities, including Muhammad Ali, Joe Namath and Joseph Barbera, the creator of *The Flintstones*, pay three thousand dollars for the pen, thus guaranteeing that it is their signature on the product you're buying.

Fast-forward a few years to when the price of those pens comes down and think about what this is going to do for all those plots involving forged paintings, documents, etc.

WRITE WHAT YOU KNOW

I'm lucky in that in writing the Nick Polo mystery series, I have an excellent source to draw on. Fellow named Jerry Keneally. He's often rather grumpy, but eventually he delivers the goods.

Nick Polo is a private eye. I've been a licensed investigator for over twenty years, so I pretty much slotted into the private eye genre.

Of course, there are genres within genres: softboiled, hardboiled, etc. I like to think of the Polo books as *al dente*.

Being a so-called real-life private investigator certainly helps me in writing the Polo books. In addition to plot possibilities, I manage to come into contact with some very interesting characters, and, like most writers, I salt these away for the time when they will fit a book just right.

I try to have Nick Polo work the way an actual private investigator does in today's world.

The days of the trench coat, shoulder-holstered .45 semi-automatic and half-filled, or half-empty, bottle of bourbon in the office desk drawer are over. I'm not sure they actually ever existed, but great writers such as Hammett and Chandler made them as real as rain.

If you are going to write a modern mystery, somewhere along the way computers, fax machines and the Internet are going to be a necessity.

I started preaching this "computer gospel" at writer's conventions and the like over ten years ago.

Back then the usual response was, "What would a PI need a computer for?"

Quite simply, without one, the real-life investigator would be out of business. The instant access to databases has changed the game dramatically and has taken away yet another of the old genre standbys: gumshoes.

In the old days our intrepid PI actually walked those mean streets. Now the investigator sits at a desk, connects the computer via modem into one of literally hundreds of databases and pulls up all kinds of background information: real property records, civil law suits on file, criminal filings, bankruptcy records, marriage and death records, reverse directories, and on and on and on.

Some PI writers shy away from computers completely, while others have the machines perform magical feats that are just impossible—my favorite is running a common name like, oh, John Taylor, and coming up with an address.

The scourge of real-life private investigators is locating someone with a common name like Taylor, or Smith, or Jones. Without a date of birth or Social Security number to pin the individual down, you're going to find a thousand John Taylors, and your client is not going to pay you to sift through them all.

The writer should pay some attention to the poor client. A real-life investigator would have a hard time making a living working for private parties. Most of us work for insurance carriers or attorneys. All too often the person who hires the fictional PI is either a rich buffoon who puts up with the PI's wisecracks or a toothsome woman who will "do anything" to get this particular private investigator to handle her case.

I think that Nero Wolfe was the only one who really could pull that scene off. In California, there are some 6,500 private investigators, so we treat our clients with great respect. Even Philip Marlowe wore his best blue suit and his socks with the clocks on them when he went to meet General Sternwood in the great opening chapter of *The Big Sleep*.

But you're writing a book. You want your investigator out of his/her office and out on those mean streets, talking to real life characters. Me too.

I am continually surprised by the responses given when I do get out there and knock on some strange door. Knock knock. A deep questioning voice will bark out, "Who is it?"

"Jerry Keneally."

Bingo, the door opens. The person on the other side of that door has no idea who Jerry Keneally is. I think I could say, "Boston Strangler," and they'd open the door and say, "Hello, Mr. Strangler."

One book had a private eye searching for someone who had a cabin in the country. To get to that cabin address, the PI had to talk a policeman and then a realtor into giving him the information that led to the wanted address. This took a full chapter, and the scenes showed the investigator's skill at conning these individuals and also introduced two new characters.

Real life—thirty seconds on the computer and you have the address.

But which version is more interesting? More entertaining? More page-turning?

There's no way you're going to be able to please everyone, as with the Scotland Yard gentlemen not appreciating P.D. James.

You'll make mistakes. Everyone does. A best-selling thriller writer's recent book had one character screwing a silencer on a revolver. A major no-no. For technical reasons involving the construction of the weapon, this just can't be done. Silencers, or sound-suppressors as the underground manufacturers call them, have to go on an automatic or semi-automatic pistol.

Did the best-selling author get any mail on this? I would think so. Your readers really care and, if you get it wrong, will let you know about your mistakes.

There are shelves of books full of background material relating to just about everything you need to know to make your novel accurate enough to please most everyone.

How do you get that information that you can't find in the library, your local bookstore or on the Web? Just ask.

It's amazing to me how cooperative people are when you identify yourself as a writer and ask for some help.

Over the years, I've queried detectives, coroners, doctors, firefighters, bookies, hang gliders, pilots, locksmiths and computer nerds, and have had very few turndowns when I've presented myself as a writer.

If I told these same individuals that I was a private investigator looking for information, most would brush me off in fear of becoming entangled in a legal tort.

In fact, if a so-called real-life private eye was smart, he'd present himself as a writer when asking his questions.

So, you've worked out your plot, you've drawn your characters, you've done your research. Everything is going fine, until suddenly—you're stuck.

FAKE THE REST

I've written myself into many a corner, and I think some of the best writing I've done is figuring a way to get out of the corner.

In a recent Polo effort, *Beggar's Choice*, I had Nick breaking into a warehouse in the South of Market district in San Francisco.

The method of breaking in was, I thought, ingenious. In fact, I created a character, a retired burglar who reformed and went into the business of advising industrial clients how not to be burgled, to get Polo through that double-locked door.

Now Nick was in the building. I had spent some time with a former member of the San Francisco Bomb Squad, picking his brain as to just what type of trap the bad guy would have waiting inside the warehouse for Polo.

The trap was set, Nick was inside, and then it dawned on me: I had to have a way for him to get back out alive.

Unfortunately, the solution came to me as these things often do, in the middle of the night. A basketball.

The bomb squad guy was impressed when he read the chapter, asking how I had come up with the idea.

I had to tell him the truth. I made it up. Faked it.

WRITING THE PI SHORT STORY

I Can Do That!

Christine Matthews

Growing up on the South Side of Chicago, I was raised by a mother who thought it was just as important that I watch Boris Karloff's performance in *Frankenstein* as Vivien Leigh's in *Gone With the Wind*. My family ate dinner while the television set was tuned to *Twilight Zone, One Step Beyond* and *Outer Limits*. Rod Serling, spewing multisyllabic words in rich, elegant tones, was the first audio influence I can remember. No one spoke like that in my neighborhood. I listened mesmerized. And then came the ending of each program and POW! I never saw it coming.

One glorious evening in 1960, my mother and aunt took my cousin and me to see a double feature at the State Theater: *13 Ghosts* and *Psycho*. The only thing I remember about *13 Ghosts* were the ghost viewer glasses, 3-D things enabling the audience to brave it out and see the ghosts, or admit cowardice and stash the cardboard goggles away.

Then *Psycho* came on. I was intrigued by Norman Bates, had never known anyone like him and yet he seemed familiar. Far more frightening than any old ghost, he was real. He could have been a brother to the strange man down the block from us who lived in the big green house. And the shock ending kept my ten-year-old self awake for nights afterwards. It was wonderful.

So began my writing career. Inspired by Rod Serling, fueled by the words as put together by Ray Bradbury, The Beatles and Aldous Huxley, I filled notebooks, scraps of paper . . . my soul. It wasn't enough to write a great story and do it elegantly; I also wanted to stun my reader. I wanted to create characters who appeared to be normal but, as each page turned, grew stranger. Not caring about genres, I ended up having more than twenty short stories published, all of which were classified as horror and dark fantasy. But I only knew I was writing about fear.

It was from this background that I went to my first mystery convention.

I've been asked why I would seek out mystery writers when I hadn't read or written mysteries. There were several reasons. First was the convenience—the convention was only a few miles from where I lived. Second, it was a chance to network with other writers. Last came the curiosity. How, I wondered, were those writers different from me? What were their fans like?

I was struck by an obvious contrast the moment I entered the lobby of the convention hotel. If you've never been to a horror convention, I'll clue you in: Wear black and lots of metal. Black leather, black nail polish, black lipstick, anything black. Studded wristbands, zippers, skull-shaped rings. Not so at a mystery convention. The men wore light-colored slacks fresh with pressed creases, sports coats, Polo shirts, even an occasional tie. The women wore pants suits or fashionable dresses. Their accessories reflected their eye for details. Beige and trendy colors were evident.

The name tags were also different than the ones I was accustomed to seeing. It took me some time to figure out that the writer's name was followed not only by his home state but by his pseudonyms and names of his fictional private investigators. And so I learned my first important fact about mystery writers and fans: They think in terms of series.

For the next few days I attended lectures and was delighted to learn about things horror writers never discuss, but should. There were panels on poisons and weapons; experts elaborated about autopsies; there was even a field trip to a morgue. These were my kind of people! Just as Norman Bates had tried to fool me into thinking he was so very "normal" (even done up as his mother he chose a conservative dress), I soon found out these well-dressed people were nice and strange.

By the third day of the convention, I had met several writers and editors. We sat in the bar and the conversation got around to an upcoming anthology of PI stories. It was agreed that I could contribute something original to the collection and so I was asked to try my hand at writing a PI story.

At first I was hesitant, but enthusiasm got the best of me and I said, "I can do that!" But during the ride home I wondered how I would redeem myself.

Conjuring up my hero, Rod Serling, for inspiration, I was suddenly struck with the memory of another favorite television program. It too had been introduced by a man who spoke in a unique voice. It also featured short stories in an anthology format but they were considered mysteries rather than tales of fantasy. Delighting me each week with surprise endings, *The Alfred Hitchcock Hour* had given me years of great memories. The only mystery series I had read was Nancy Drew, but when I was older I had liked *The Rockford Files*. He was a private investigator, right? Maybe I did have some knowledge of the mystery genre. Besides, a good writer can write anything, I assured myself.

Mulling over my predicament, I spotted the Stephen Vincent Benet quote tacked above my desk: "A short story is something that can be read in an hour and remembered for a lifetime."

My objective was the same it had always been—to write a memorable story. Accomplishing it would require techniques I had not used before. And so I prepared myself much the same way I had when I started writing horror—I watched, I read and I studied what was out there. It took considerable time and effort; unfortunately there was no book like the one you are now holding for me to refer to. Contained within the next few pages is what I learned. I hope you will benefit from my research.

WHO IS THIS PI PERSON?

If you want to write a private eye story, you had better know what a private eye is. According to Robert J. Randisi, founder of the Private Eye Writers of America and the author of the Nick Delvecchio and Miles Jacoby private eye series, a private eye is "a man or woman who gets paid for investigating. He/she does not belong to any law enforcement agency." A license is usually in the PI's wallet, but is not necessary. Two examples of nonlicensed PIs are: Lawrence Block's Matthew Scudder, an ex-cop, and William Tappley's Brady Coyne, a lawyer who also becomes involved with his own investigations.

The private eye is able to defend himself. In my reading I found that while some investigators favor a certain type of weapon, others have an aversion to them. The latter seem to rely more on their wits and humor or have been trained in some sort of martial art.

But most important of all, private eyes, be they female or male, are real people.

I had a hard time with this. The main character in a contemporary horror story has to be real . . . except for one thing. And it's that one thing that the reader will buy only if you, as a writer, have created a sympathetic character.

In Stephen King's *The Dark Half*, an author, writing under a pseudonym, appears pretty ordinary. He starts getting calls from his alter ego, created in the literary world. The reader is led to believe the threat resides only in the writer's imagination. But when people start getting murdered, it becomes evident the dark half is real; somehow, this ordinary man managed to unleash his evil self in tangible form.

It was always with the idea of the "except for" factor that I created my main character. And as I began reading PI fiction, I expected to find a lot of dames in tight dresses and guys wrapped in trenchcoats, but I never expected to identify with any of them. What a surprise, then, to discover private investigators who reminded me of people I knew. Even myself. People struggling to pay bills, keep their families together or just get a good night's sleep. Nothing lurking beneath the skin, they were real—through and through. Except for . . . nothing. There were no inconsistencies.

Since my story was to appear in *Deadly Allies II*, I thought it best to read through the first *Deadly Allies*. Below are some examples of the humanity I found between the covers.

V.I. Warshawski, Sara Paretsky's PI, lost her mother to cancer and was an aggressive athlete while still in high school. As an adult, she likes Greek food and prefers to keep her gun locked in a safe in her bedroom.

Alo Nudger, created by John Lutz, chomps down antacids and has his office above Danny's Donuts. Danny makes horrible donuts but Nudger eats them rather than insult his friend.

Sue Grafton's Kinsey Millhone works out at a gym and worries about where she should do her banking.

WHO ARE THESE CLIENTS?

While the PI is the reliable thread running through a story, his client can be outrageous, a liar, even a murderer. The movies I saw as a kid left me with black-and-white impressions of eccentric, rich, troubled people desperate for help. Hiring a private investigator was expensive, a luxury only for the upper class. But after mentally rerunning my favorite *Rockford Files* episodes, I remembered Jim's clients as middle class, sometimes unable to even pay him for his trouble.

My reading confirmed that the last half of the twentieth century seemed to have offered the modern PI a wider variety of clients who in turn brought with them more relevant problems. From abused housewives to enthusiastic activists, they knocked on glass doors and sat awkwardly in old chairs looking to our hero for help.

But no matter who they were or where they came from, every client had to be willing to pay for the PI's services.

HOW MUCH?

The average going rate charged by your modern day investigator seems to be two hundred dollars a day plus expenses. In a recent episode of *Mike Hammer*, Stacy Keach got paid twenty dollars an hour.

LOCALE

I've heard mystery writers say that the PI's city should be just as important to the story as its characters. From the start, a private eye usually lived and worked in either California or New York. A few authors wrote about other cities in the seventies, but it wasn't until the 1980s that writers embraced the places they knew best.

Loren D. Estleman wrote about Detroit in 1980 in *Motor City Blues*. Jeremiah Healy wrote about Boston; Sara Paretsky lived in Chicago and wrote about her town. The readers loved being taken on vicarious trips through the streets of places they either knew or would like to visit. The more details, the better. But remember, when your shamus turns right on a street, make sure it isn't one-way going in the opposite direction. Readers will feel cheated and let you know about any discrepancies.

Les Roberts moved from Los Angeles to his adopted home-town of Cleveland, Ohio. Now Cleveland is just as much of a star as his private eye, Milan Jacovich. I've visited Les's home and seen copies of the top ten fiction best-seller lists in Cleveland. His sales outrank Tom Clancy's and John Grisham's. Cleveland natives love what Les has done for their city and they show it by buying his novels.

THE CRIME

A crime has to take place somewhere along the way in a PI story. There can be a robbery, kidnapping or jewel heist, but most readers like a murder thrown in. Once the crime has been committed, or a hint of one has been whiffed, the perpetrators must be brought to justice. These are morality tales. Your PI is the hero, the one in the white hat.

ACTION

Even in this age of the fax machine, e-mail and computers, your private investigator must still physically move around. He has to interview, follow and apprehend. In my research I found that a PI calls on each suspect an average of two times within the framework of a short story. The first visit is taken up with introductions, basic questions or just notification that something has happened. Perhaps someone has been reported missing or has been threatened. The second visit is to double-check the original story as well as to confront the suspect with new evidence.

While it is possible to write a story using clues gotten by mechanical means, it's the face-to-face visits that allow the writer a chance to describe characters, develop the PI and offer more scenery.

Then comes stalking, some skulking and the chase. Your shamus can move on foot, in a car, on a subway—be creative.

DON'T FORGET THE BASICS

John Lutz wrote: "The best thing about today's PI fiction is that it is no longer so constricted by formula . . . the only criterion for categorization as PI fiction now is that the story's main character . . . is [a] private detective."

No matter what the genre, there's no getting around the fact that you'll be using the same basic ingredients (description, characterization, dialogue, action, etc.) you used when writing other short stories. Unlike a novel that allows the writer pages to wander, a short story must be, by virtue of its own definition, short. You only have room for one main plot, and if you're very adept, one subplot. Keep it simple. Remember, your purpose is to pack one single, emotional punch.

You've seen the famous last scene in so many horror flicks. The monster is killed, or thought to be destroyed, and as the camera watches our leading man exit the scene, his arm cinched around his horrified girlfriend, the monster's eye twitches. Or a hand jerks up from a grave. The poor hero thought he saved the world. But we know the truth. And that knowledge fills us with apprehension. The horror fan is supposed to leave the book or movie with his heart pounding, looking over his shoulder, his mind crazy with the fear.

Not so for mystery fans. They want a hero in the private

investigator. No matter how human, he has to be out there chasing down the crooks. And when he kills the bad guys, they stay dead. When he turns a thief over to the police, the streets—our streets—are safe again. There must be a resolution at the end of this type of story. It is therefore, very important that you have a beginning, a middle and an ending in a PI short story.

Of course there are exceptions, there are always exceptions; no rule goes unbroken.

In Robert J. Randisi's novel *The Steinway Collection*, private investigator Miles Jacoby is hired to recover a prize collection of pulp detective magazines. The book ends without the collection being found.

We all know that every police department and private investigator has a pile of unsolved cases. But mystery readers were upset, and they told the author so whenever they met him at conventions.

When I started writing my weird stories, an editor told me writing in the first person was a no-no. He went on to explain that in order to build the suspense I wanted, writing the type of fiction I wrote, it was necessary to show the reader what danger lay ahead, around the corner. I had to create my monster, be it real or imagined, give it a separate life from the main character and yet make it just as viable. External forces, unseen by my character, also figured in. The mood I wanted to set from the start was one of trepidation. So, no matter how much I wanted to write in first person, I trained myself to paint the big picture, take my reader one step back so they could see all the evil lurking.

While doing my own research to write my first PI story, I couldn't help but notice that PI stories were all, with very few exceptions, written in that first person voice. The tone set from the start was one of intimacy; I was seeing things at the same time and from the same perspective as the hero. This technique also offered some insight into the mind of the PI.

The short story is tight, dense and compact. Choice of the

right word in the right place is important. There is no room for fat. But while my horror tales ran between thirteen and twenty pages, the PI stories have gone as long as forty. It just takes more space to introduce a crisis, develop the detective and crack the case.

BE SURE YOU KNOW WHAT YOU'RE WRITING

I was rejected by an editor once because, as he explained it, "This is an excellent story; however, we don't know what it is you have written."

In the horror genre there is only one subgenre I can think of: dark fantasy. I am sure there may be a few others but none come to mind. Years ago, I went to purchase *The Dead Zone* at a local book store. The horror section was considerably smaller than it is today; in fact it was nonexistent. That would explain why the book was shelved in the "suspense" section and why Edgar Allan Poe was found in "literature." So imagine my total confusion when I started reading mysteries only to find so many different types. As near as I can count, there are seven subgenres under the "mystery" umbrella. Below is a breakdown and a famous name associated with each to help you keep them straight.

1. PI—Mickey Spillane
2. Cozy—Agatha Christie
3. Suspense—Mary Higgins Clark
4. Police Procedural—Ed McBain
5. Crime Novels—Donald Westlake (writing as Richard Stark)
6. Legal Thriller—John Grisham
7. Amateur Sleuth—Jessica Fletcher (fictional writer of Murder, She Wrote)

The fact that there are so many working parts of the mystery genre seems to me at first confusing, then liberating, then mystifying. While a horror writer may write about ghosts, or vampires, or the cannibal living next door, his stories are all considered "horror." Why does the mystery field feel it necessary to classify and classify again?

By dividing, are they creating more markets and specialized magazines in which to be published?

Then again, the mystery genre encompasses so much, why branch off and alienate readers or writers in any way?

One of the most powerful books I have read in the past few years is Thomas Harris's *The Silence of the Lambs*. I remember the convention I was at, the seat I was in when listening to a panel discussing this writer and his great "horror" novel. A few years later I was talking with some mystery writers and noticed that they spoke about Thomas Harris's wonderful "thriller." While one set of friends analyzed the character of the horrific Hannibal Lecter, the other concentrated on the FBI agent, Clarice Starling.

And what about my all-time favorite movie, *Psycho*? It wasn't until a PI writer I know commented on how much he enjoyed the private investigator in that movie that I remembered the part played by Martin Balsam.

No matter which character you choose to focus on, would that book and movie be classified as "horror," a "psychological thriller," or "suspense"? Even if you don't think in terms of genre, editors and publishers do. So, when writing a mystery of any kind, keep in mind what it is you're writing and who your audience is. It has been predicted that within the next ten years there will be even more subgenres. The latest trend? Church lady mysteries.

STARTING

Having completed my research, getting it straight in my mind what elements went into a PI story, I then had to dream up a plot.

Every writer gets asked where they get their ideas. And most often, when they are asked, eyes roll and fingers start tapping with irritation. For when I say writers get asked this question *a lot*, I mean by every interviewer, every student and every fan. At every workshop, convention and chance meeting.

Considering the complexities of the human brain, I can see why everyone is so interested. Trying to understand what stokes the creative flames can be even more intriguing. But, no matter how different we like to consider ourselves from every other human being on earth, it's a cruel fact that we are all made of the same stuff. What starts me thinking is probably the same things that start you up, or your brother, or his friend.

Easy to understand, then, that it was something as mundane as a television talk show that was the inspiration behind my first PI story. And it was the lyrics from one of my favorite songs that inspired the title for "Gentle Insanities."

Phil Donahue was doing a program about unusual occupations. There was a female PI on the panel. She commented that a person would have to be a little crazy to be a private investigator. I started there, with a woman who finds herself in an occupation she considers just a job, a way to pay the bills.

Because I was new to the genre, I decided to make Roberta Stanton a newcomer to her field. That way, I figured, we could learn together. I furnished her office with desks I had known in secretarial jobs and populated it with people I had worked with. I set the story in Omaha simply because I was living in that city at the time. Because I have a terrible memory, I gave Roberta (Robbie) my own likes and dislikes; I even gave her my family. And it was the same family situation I was trying to deal with that I handed over to Robbie. Her problems with my parents led to an unusual subplot and ending.

I sweated over the ending, unsure if I was crossing some forbidden boundary. When I told my editor how I planned to finish my story, he encouraged me to continue.

IN CONCLUSION

Deadly Allies II came out in April of 1994; my story was singled out as one of the unique ones. Since that time I have written many other mysteries and have been very grateful for the chance to express myself in this genre. But not much has changed.

I notice my ideas coming from the same places as they did before: television, newspaper articles, curious facts I collect in journals, memorable quotes, even gossip. It is the same strange people I choose to write about, only now they have become the supporting cast rather than the main characters.

When I was asked why I wrote horror, I would smile and say, "Because life is horrible." Unfortunately that statement seems to apply to writing about crime also. More horrifying and real than any old vampire or werewolf, we all have been a victim or know someone who has been. Maybe ideas for your PI stories will come from sources closer to home than expected.

My last piece of advice in helping you prepare to write a good private eye short story is: Listen.

You're going to be writing about real people, real problems, real emotions. Listen to conversations in malls, listen to not only the accents but the fears expressed, the way they are conveyed. Listen to stories friends tell about their relatives or their children; listen to news reports, talk shows, CNN. Cop shows are good sources for crime scenes. Be interested in everything. The original topic may not catch your attention but something said by just one person can trigger off story ideas, characters and dialogue. A mystery writer no longer has the luxury of locking himself away in a garret and creating; those times are long gone. Nowadays you have to network and research.

After you've read this entire book through, you'll be left with more information than you know what to do with. Don't worry. Just remember that good writing is good writing, no matter what the genre. It's all a matter of how you approach your subject and in which direction you plan to travel.

Short and Shamus

John Lutz

A good private eye short story is a good short story and then some. Writing PI short fiction requires all the skills of the short story writer, along with the ability to plant clues, foreshadow (not the same as planting clues), create an interesting clash of adversaries, and instill in the story the most neglected of the four main elements of fiction: theme.

Theme, which can be defined as simply what a story means, is especially important in PI fiction because usually at base we are spinning tales of morality. Simple and overused themes such as the premise that good shall, for whatever reasons, inevitably triumph, or that criminals always make one potentially fatal mistake, are still usable if given a fresh twist and employed cleverly enough. But mystery readers have become more sophisticated and now demand more. Writers and publishers should, in fact in the long run *must*, accommodate this more savvy, flexible and demanding reader.

Generally speaking, writing a good short story is more difficult than writing a good novel, but there are a few advantages the short story writer enjoys. One is that there are story ideas unsuitable for the novel form, but that might be ideal for the short story.

An example is the classic by the great short story writer Stanley Ellin "The Question My Son Asked" (first published in *Ellery Queen's Mystery Magazine*, November, 1962). The story concerns a professional executioner who is passing along his very specialized occupation to his son. The proud father explains the need for such a profession, the responsibility and overriding morality, and teaches his son to treat the task with respect, diligence and dignity. There is a sacred bond of trust between father and son, a tradition of absolute truth with each other, and everything goes smoothly until the son asks the one question his father has dreaded: "You enjoy it, don't you?"

The father is compelled to answer honestly.

Whether or not you agree with the answer, you'll enjoy and admire the story. But obviously a novel building up over three hundred pages to such a simple question and answer would be overkill.

From the writer's point of view, the best thing about today's PI fiction is that it is no longer so constricted by formula. Molds have been broken during the past ten or fifteen years, and the only criterion for categorization as PI fiction now is that the story or novel's main character, or at least *a* main character, is a private detective. And even the definition of private detective has been stretched. Books and stories using PI fiction tenets (and stretching or breaking them) often feature as investigators journalists, social workers, attorneys, medical doctors, even historical figures and medieval monks.

Still, when you conceive and develop your story idea, it's best to keep in mind that, as in virtually all good fiction, you will want to make your PI protagonist a sympathetic character, one with whom the reader can identify. He or she should become enmeshed in an interesting situation in a plausible and intriguing setting. And when the story is ended, it should all have meant something that is, if not profound, at least satisfactory and in some way meaningful, both for the PI and the reader.

Of the four main elements of fiction—character, setting, situation and theme—except in rare instances, the primary one should be character. Most good fiction is rooted in character, and this seems to be especially true of good PI fiction, from Sherlock Holmes to Kinsey Millhone.

Whether you work from an outline or simply a mental framework—or if you plot as you go along, as some very accomplished writers do—it's always a good idea to check the four main elements of fiction and make sure they're strong enough to give the story plausibility and impetus. Your character must face a main problem and encounter conflict as the story progresses through stages of increasing pressure, obstacles and/or suspense, culminating in a crisis, climax and anticlimax.

And of course like all skilled short story writers you must use techniques for writing short rather than simply writing in condensed form. That means being able to get the reader into the story quickly by introducing your characters and main problem much earlier and more compactly than in a novel. A short story writer has only a sentence or a paragraph to accomplish what a novelist might do in a page or even a chapter, whether it's to establish character, strike reality into a setting or lay out the mechanism of the story in a believable and gripping fashion.

In the short story, this compression is accomplished by making almost everything serve more than one purpose. Description of setting and situation might also suggest something about a character. Dialogue might reveal something about the character speaking as well as the character being spoken about, and provide information that advances the story and maybe even plants a clue. Here's an example from one of my own stories, "The Real Shape of the Coast" (first published in *Ellery Queen's Mystery Magazine* in June 1971). The setting, a seaside state institution for the criminally insane, has been introduced, and one of the patients has been found dead on the beach. The first words spoken:

> "This simply won't do," the doctor was saying. "One of
> you has done away with Mr. Rolt, and that is exactly the
> sort of thing we are in here to stop."

The reader has obtained information here. It is assumed that one of the inmates murdered Rolt. The doctor's merely annoyed, patronizing tone establishes the relationship between the patients and staff. And the story's main problem has been introduced—murder won't be tolerated, so this one must be solved.

In this story, the detective (a PI in the liberal sense of the term) is Logan, another inmate, incarcerated after being found guilty of murdering his wife by bludgeoning her with a wine bottle. Though he's not being paid and is working mainly for himself, it is Logan who is our investigator and who must solve this crime alone. His reaction to another inmate's reminder that Logan murdered his wife:

> "I warn you," Logan said heatedly, "implying that I struck my wife with a wine bottle—and French Chablis at that— is inviting a libel suit!"

This not only lets the reader know that Logan maintains his innocence, it emphasizes Logan's insanity by illustrating that his priorities are scrambled. And it lays the groundwork for his antagonistic relationship with another inmate. His vehement denial of guilt also makes plausible his motive to act as a detective. Logan again: "Justice must be done. Rolt's murderer—a real murderer—must be caught and executed."

So his motivation springs from character—Logan's desperate refusal to see himself as a killer. When reminded by the doctor that the investigation is a job for the police, Logan replies: "The police! . . . Look how they botched my case!"

Logan expresses again that he is innocent of murdering his wife, and his distrust of the police further establishes that he must act as the detective to get to the bottom of Rolt's murder. In a few short passages of dialogue, the main character, situation and setting have been defined, motivation has been explained, and the tone of the story has been established.

An editor once complimented a short story writer by saying he could write *War and Peace* on the back of an envelope. He didn't mean the writer would condense the novel. He meant the writer had the ability to smoothly and unobtrusively use his prose for more than one purpose while engaging the reader's emotions. And that, in the last analysis, is what writing good fiction is all about—engaging the reader's emotions. If you can accomplish that, everything else will fall into place. This is just as true of the PI short story as of other types of short fiction.

In the PI story the writer has some additional challenges. Whether the story is written in first person or in third, usually the reader finds and analyzes clues along with the detective, yet we can't allow the reader to solve the case *before* the PI. So the PI story should be written in such a way that at the end it will seem to the reader that had he or she been just a little sharper or more observant, the solution to the crime would have been foreseen. The story has to end with the reader thinking "Of course!" as well as "Ah-ha!" A sort of mental snapping of the fingers, as if something elusive barely managed to slip past, but wouldn't have had we been slightly quicker or more observant. Of course the truth is that if the writer has done a proper job, it only *seems* that way.

One of the special skills the PI writer needs to accomplish this is the planting of clues. Here the short story writer's technique of using almost everything for more than one purpose gains an added dimension. Clues might be almost unnoticeably included within other matter, but in that case must at the same time be obtrusive enough to be recalled during the story's resolution. A delicate balancing act.

In the planting of a red herring, a clue might be introduced obviously (but not so obviously that it is a red herring), in order to mislead the reader.

Another technique is to present a clue obviously, but as something else.

Here's an example of the first technique, a clue presented along with other matter, from my story "Someone Else" (published in *Justice For Hire*, edited by Robert J. Randisi, Mysterious Press, 1990):

He roamed about, saw a desk in Garnett's office. The drawers yielded nothing other than the usual household correspondence and a few innocuous business letters. The bookshelf behind the desk contained automotive manuals and a stack of paperback western novels. On the desk's corner was a small empty brass picture frame; probably it had contained the photo of Gloria Garnett that her husband had shown to Carver when he'd hired him. . . .

The clue here is the empty picture frame, but mention of it is preceded by phrases like "nothing other than the usual" and "a few innocuous," and it is merely one of a number of items mentioned, some of which suggest more likely clues, as the frame which is "probably" the one that held the photo shown to Carver by his client. So it is unobtrusively yet memorably presented, so that when it turns out to have been a clue, the reader will recall it (reinforced as it is later with more, this time hidden, empty picture frames) and not feel cheated.

An example of a red herring (a false and misleading clue) is in Sir Arthur Conan Doyle's famous Sherlock Holmes story "The Red-headed League." Mr. Jabez Wilson is a pawnbroker who has answered a newspaper ad inviting "All red-headed men who are sound in body and mind and above the age of twenty-one years" to apply for a well paying job requiring only "nominal services." Mr. Jabez, who has flaming red hair, is chosen to fill this vacancy. His duties are only to copy the *Encyclopedia Britannica* for an organization called the Red-headed League.

Of course, the reader, along with Mr. Jabez and Dr. Watson, is concentrating on the fact that his red hair, and The Red-headed League itself, must have some important meaning, when in fact Mr. Jabez didn't get the position because of his red hair at all. The position and the League were created expressly for him in order to get him away from his pawnshop each morning so its cellar can be used to tunnel into a nearby bank vault. So in this instance, even the story's title turns out to be a misleading clue, a classic "red" herring.

Part of the art of planting red herrings is to be subtle, yet obvious enough for the reader to assume he or she is seeing through your subterfuge. The reader senses that there's something other than the obvious in the bizarre Red-headed League, but doesn't suspect that the entire red-headed aspect, including the title, is a diversion and not what the story revolves around.

In another Holmes work, *A Study in Scarlet*, we have a clue presented as something else. At the scene of a murder, the word *Rache* has been scrawled in blood on a wall above the corpse. The reader might assume that before death the victim attempted to write the name *Rachel* in his own blood but was too weak to complete it. Through most of the story, the reader is waiting for a woman named Rachel to appear, or for someone to be involved with a Rachel. In fact, the blood turns out to be that of the murderer (from a nosebleed), and the name *Rachel* isn't involved. The word on the wall is complete: *Rache* is German for *Revenge*.

Foreshadowing is different from planting clues. In fiction, especially the short story, everything must mean something, and coincidence doesn't happen as it might in real life. For instance, if your PI is in danger and suddenly uses a Swiss Army knife to remove hinge screws and escape captivity, though the reader will accept that the PI *might* have been carrying a Swiss Army knife (ah-ha!), its appearance will still border on the contrived. The knife must be shown to the reader in an earlier scene; maybe the PI will use it to open a package or clean his fingernails. A female PI might use the pocket knife as a key fob so she can locate it easily in her purse. And *if* the knife is shown, it should later reappear or be of some significance in the story. The showing of the knife is the foreshadowing of the later scene, when it is used to remove the hinge screws (of course!).

This example of foreshadowing is from another of my PI short stories, "Without Anchovies" (first published in *Murder Is My Business*, edited by Mickey Spillane and Max Allan Collins, Dutton, 1994). Hapless PI Ralph Hamish, thinking he is taking part in a practical joke, has mistakenly struck the local organized crime boss Paul Marin in the face with a pizza, and is later visited in his office by Marin's sadistic sons:

"Paul Marin is your father?" Hamish said.

"Unfortunately for you," Crush said, "that's true. He's a

man would kill either one of us if we hit him in the face with a pizza. I mean, he put me in the hospital for a week when I was sixteen 'cause I put a dent in the car. You can imagine what he wants done with you."

"He'd rather not," Jack said. He leveled his gun and casually blasted Hamish's telephone. The shattering plastic made more noise than the shot.

"That thing under warranty or anything?" Crush asked.

Hamish shook his head no.

"My brother had some trouble with federal people tapping his phone," Crush explained. "'Cause of that, he doesn't like phones, so whenever he gets a chance, he drills one. I guess that's better than where his next shot might go, huh?'"

Telephones, and phone taps, have been foreshadowed. The reader is presented with the fact that Hamish is in mortal danger in the paragraph preceding when the phone is shot. One of the thugs shooting a phone on the desk is a surprise to the reader, something that engages emotion and will lodge in the memory. So the reader won't suspect it is of any importance, we distract him with some humor, Crush's question about a warranty. Then we supply an explanation for why Jack shot the phone: his anger over his own phone being tapped by federal agents. As far as the reader knows, in having Jack blast the phone, the writer has only been going for shock value and the comic touch.

It is later now in the story, after Hamish has gotten used to the idea that the city's criminal element now consider him a crime kingpin, and has even come to so enjoy his new status that he's come out of hiding and returned to town and his office:

The first thing he noticed when he walked into his office was the new phone. Probably a gift, he figured, a gesture of respect from his men. The second thing he noticed was the envelope containing the fifty thousand dollars. He picked it up. . . .

We've mentioned the phone again, followed by the immediate distraction of the envelope and fifty thousand dollars. A few paragraphs down the same page, the phone is back:

> The phone rang. Sort of chimed, actually. A chime of respect.
> Hamish picked up the clean white receiver, noticing it was heavy. An expensive phone. He said hello.

The caller, Jack Marin, makes it clear to Hamish that he is no kingpin at all, explaining how he's going to see that it's known that his dead brother Crush killed the people Hamish is given credit for rubbing out, even though Jack and Crush both killed them. Crush, being dead, is beyond the law's reach and so will make an ideal patsy. The object will be to establish that Hamish *isn't* a tough killer at all, so that a hood named Bigger Lou will surely kill him:

> "So long, Hamish," Jack said with a nasty little chuckle. "Either here or in Cincinnati, where you thought you were hiding out, you're a dead man that just needs a place to lie down. Or maybe you should try some other city. You don't think Bigger Lou can track you down within hours. You're dead wrong." He laughed. "It don't matter if he can spell the place or not, he's got ways to find you wherever you go."
> Click. Buzz.
> The connection was broken.

Some humor to distract again, along with mention of the phone when Jack hung up. Hamish is on the run again, until he learns the city's crime organization has been broken, and police lieutenant Malloy explains how:

> "It's all about you, Ralph," Malloy said. "The case against Jack Marin is based on the wiretap recording of his phone

conversation with you."

"Me?" Then Hamish remembered the new phone in his office, replacing the one Jack Marin had shot. "So it was the law that replaced my phone," he said, "not my men."

The purpose of all of the above is to show how the all-important phone was worked into the story in ways that kept it alive in the reader's unconscious, in order to achieve the desired "Ah, ha! Of course!" when the new phone turns out to be Hamish's means of salvation.

Another important and often overlooked element in PI fiction, short and long, is the chemistry between the detective and his adversary. The writer shouldn't stop after creating an interesting hero; an interesting villain is also a plus. But it's even more of a plus if the villain and hero have a special relationship. Think of this as the flip side of the chemistry needed in a good love story. In my Carver stories, Carver, like all private detectives in the classic mold, religiously tries to follow his strict ethical code. Because of this, he is often at odds with police lieutenant William McGregor, who is not only corrupt but admits it and gleefully wallows in his corruption. Carver is cursed to struggle with moral dilemma, but McGregor has made his deal with the devil long ago and is happily unencumbered by morality or conscience. That they live according to opposite philosophies makes for more interesting confrontations between them. Their conflict with each other stems as much from character as from external causes.

My fictional PI Nudger is an inversion of the classic PI. He is frightened often; loathes firearms; has a nervous stomach, a suicidal girlfriend and a humble office above a doughnut shop (it is occasionally remarked upon that he smells like a dough-nut); and does whatever he can to avoid danger. He is in the wrong business and knows it but cannot escape it because he is unqualified for any other occupation and desperately needs the money. So, gentle and nonconfrontational soul that he is, he continues in his tentative way to walk the mean streets. In the short story "Before You Leap" (*Deadly Allies*, edited by Robert J. Randisi, Doubleday, 1992), Nudger meets his opposite number, a villain named Nubber who is also a private detective and for whom Nudger has been mistaken. This polarity in personalities and situations is drawn in the two paragraphs where Nudger goes to see Nubber in his office:

> Nubber had a classy waiting room. A classy receptionist, who took Nudger's name, spoke into an intercom, then ushered him into a large, high-ceilinged office with a mammoth antique desk beneath a slowly revolving paddle fan. This would impress clients, Nudger thought, and Nubber wouldn't smell like a Dunker Delite and scare them away by seeming low class and high in cholesterol.
>
> Nubber himself was seated behind the desk wearing a black-and-white-checkered sport jacket and a yellow tie. He was a smiling, bland-faced man, but with glittering dark eyes that gave him the look of the tiger. He seemed the sort who should be hawking used cars or life insurance rather than working as a private detective. The tennis court-size desk made Nubber look smaller. When he stood up, Nudger saw that he was about his size—just under six feet tall—though a bit on the pudgy side. Well, Nudger was getting a little pudgy himself.

While describing the office and Nubber above, the paragraphs emphasize the differences in Nudger and Nubber despite the similarities in their names and a superficial physical resemblance. It is Nudger who envies the spacious and luxurious office that smacks of success, so unlike his own. It is Nubber who has "the look of the tiger." It is hoped that the reader will anticipate not only trouble but trouble of an interesting nature between these two opposing figures and read on. And prompting readers to read on is the object of our game.

An effective short story is exactly that, whichever category it falls into, and wherever you might find it in a library or bookstore or magazine rack. An effective private eye short story will have all the qualities of good short fiction, and in addition will feature artistry in foreshadowing, theme and the planting of clues and will involve a chemistry that adds interest and meaning to the clash of hero and villain.

The way to write a good PI story is first to read good PI stories, then read them again and analyze them. Note how the writers have established the above four important elements in the stories—character, situation, setting and theme—so that you can employ some of the same techniques.

At the same time, don't feel constricted by the old rules in this, the new golden age of mysteries. Readers, like writers (and editors), are always looking for something fresh and exciting.

After writing your story, examine it to make sure it's strong enough not only in the four basic elements of virtually all fiction, but also in the essential PI fiction elements: an intriguing crime or problems, foreshadowing, the planting of clues, interesting chemistry between PI and quarry, and an ending that is both plausible and satisfying. If it doesn't meet this criteria, try to figure out where it falls short, so that you can improve it before an editor reads it and learns of your crimes of omission.

Once the first draft is written, the secret of creating good PI short stories is in doing sound analysis—detective work—then solving the crime. It's well worth the effort.

One way or the other, the writer is the one who has to serve the sentence.

STRETCHING THE BOUNDARIES

Crossing Over

Wendi Lee

When writers sit down to write a novel, a screenplay or a short story, the first thing they must determine is what kind of story they want to tell. Most of the time, a writer thinks in terms of one genre—mystery, western romance, horror, etc. But can you combine 'em? Of course you can.

In the past ten to fifteen years, the television and movie industry has been more accepting of the cross-genre story. On TV in the early eighties, for example, *Kolchak: The Night Stalker* was a popular series about a reporter who got involved in weird supernatural cases. Today, *The X-Files* is a popular television show, with a mix of mystery and supernatural.

In feature films, *Alien Nation*, which married science fiction to the police procedural, became so popular that today it still has a cult following and has been continued as a series of novels and made-for-TV movies. Not all cross-genre movies have been successful, however. *The Valley of Gwangi* was a dinosaur-western that had a wide release—but public taste is fickle, and it fizzled at the box office. If I had known about it at the time, I certainly would have been the first person in line for a ticket if the movie had played in my neighborhood theater.

Cross-genre has always been a hard sell. Before I wrote my first novel, I had always assumed my first book would be a mystery—perhaps a suspense novel, maybe a "woman in jeopardy" plot, or possibly a cozy. But I never dreamed that when I sold my first novel in 1988, it would be a western.

Although I grew up on TV westerns like *Maverick*, *Laredo* and *Rawhide*, I also watched *The Avengers*, *The Prisoner*, *The Wild Wild West* and *The Saint*. My first novel had all the elements of a traditional western—including a "good guy, bad guy" plot—but with a main character who was a private investigator in the Old West, nothing can change the fact that my first novel was cross-genre.

Why did I do it? At the time, I wanted to write a mystery, but the market for contemporary mysteries, especially female private eyes, was in a down cycle. One day, I was on the phone with a successfully published fellow writer, and he suggested that I try to write a western. At the time, editors at publishing houses were, he said, desperate for good traditional westerns. Since I never back down from a challenge, I tried my hand at writing one. I realized that the Pinkertons were a successful investigative agency back in the 1800s, and I thought, since I couldn't write a contemporary private eye novel, how about one with a featured character who was a Pinkerton-like agent?

And I was successful. Successful enough, in fact, to continue the character in another book, then a third, until I had written six westerns featuring Jefferson Birch, a private eye in the Old West. I had unwittingly created a cross-genre series.

If I had studied the market back then, I would have come to realize that most cross-genre books or series of books were difficult to sell. Ten years ago, editors weren't sure how to sell cross-genre to the marketing and publicity people, the marketing and publicity people weren't sure how to sell it to the regional sales reps, and the sales reps weren't sure how to sell it to the bookstore managers, who weren't sure under which category to shelve the book and how to sell it to their readers.

Perhaps I was one of the lucky cross-genre writers. My western editor was always aware that my series was cross-genre, and she encouraged me to talk it up in mystery circles. In fact, my publisher, Walker and Company, was originally a mystery house that had recently expanded to include other categories. For the next few years, my cross-genre books were shelved in the western sections in bookstores and libraries. I soon found that there was no way of crossing the boundaries from western to mystery, much as I tried.

Today, cross-genre novels aren't unusual to find, and the

above-mentioned marketing and publicity, sales and bookstore people are double-shelving it. Editors are becoming more interested in reading something different, something that they might be able to sell as cross-genre. The private eye character is versatile—his or her profession can be set in most other category fiction: horror, science fiction, westerns, historicals and even fantasy can work with a featured private investigator. There has even been at least one romance novel featuring a female private eye!

There are several factors that must be addressed when writing the cross-genre PI novel: setting, tone and character. Since there are very few cross-genre PI novels out there, I've taken the liberty of using other types of cross-genre novels as examples.

SETTING

When I sat down to write my western private eye novel, I had to keep in mind the fact that I was primarily writing a western. My character, Jefferson Birch, was a private investigator in the Old West. Being a Texan in the 1870s, Birch can't wear a trenchcoat and fedora, but he can wear a duster and a Stetson. He can't carry a Magnum, but he does carry a Navy Colt. He doesn't drive a battered car, but he does have a reliable horse, Cactus.

Where you set your story is as important as the plot and characters. In a sense, the setting becomes a character in itself. Where would Sam Spade be without San Francisco? Where would Marlowe be without Los Angeles, and Spenser without Boston? You should keep foremost in your mind that your setting is a sidekick to your PI.

Time is also part of the setting. If you drop your PI into a science fiction or fantasy setting, it's even more important to remember to combine elements of the hardboiled PI with the more exotic science fiction location. There are no equivalents to the Chrysler Building in space. The backdrop has to come alive to a reader who has no reference points.

Alien Nation became a series of novels. The basic premise

is that aliens have emigrated to Earth and are made welcome by some humans, but made unwelcome by many more—it's a new form of prejudice, which is an interesting concept in itself. The setting, in which the alien Tenctonese, or "Newcomer," characters must integrate into human society, is as significant as the crime that must be solved by the human detectives, Sikes and his partner, Francisco, a Newcomer on the police force.

In *Alien Nation: Extreme Prejudice*, by L.A. Graf, the setting becomes clear by page four.

> The plane was filled with Newcomers, jostling about just like human passengers, squirming to join Sikes in the aisle, struggling to open the overhead compartments or free their luggage from under adjoining seats. Their smooth, spotted heads looked unreal against a backdrop of airplane windows covered with falling snow, and the soft click and hush of their excited words sounded like some Japanese recording played backwards and very slow. A rail-thin Newcomer female, her spots as fine as leopard skin, skittered into the aisle ahead of a tall, broad Newcomer male who was probably her mate.

The above description lets the reader know that the setting is clearly science fiction, but is set in a not-too-distant future. Later in the book, there's an exchange over breakfast at a hotel restaurant between Matt Sikes, George Francisco and Francisco's wife, Susan—the Newcomers are served tender young grasshoppers and raw, marinated weasel over a slice of cantaloupe, and Sikes responds to Francisco's complaints about the human's idea of Newcomer food:

> Across the table, Sikes glowered at his own plate, on which two eggs, a sausage link, and a strip of bacon had been combined into a vacuously smiling face. "Be grateful. At least you didn't get the rugrat special."
>
> Susan looked up from her breakfast in surprise. "Matt,

you never told us you liked rat."

The human groaned and buried his face in a cup of coffee, as if the effort of explaining had just exceeded his sleep-deprived capability. George kindly did it for him. "I believe Matthew was referring to the intended consumers of the dish, and not its contents," he told his wife.

This passage reminds the reader that the setting is not present day but a future Earth by familiarizing us with the cultural differences between humans and the Tenctonese.

On the other hand, in my Jefferson Birch series, I have to keep the setting consistent with what it must have been like in the 1870s west. In the second paragraph of *Outlaw's Fortune*, I describe the conductor as a train pulls in:

Later [Murchison] would have to put on his long, double-breasted frock coat when it was time to punch tickets on the train. Inside the cars would be hot, but for now, he could relax on the platform as the train pulled in and he directed passengers, answered questions about timetables, and supervised the porters as they unloaded and loaded luggage.

I tried to convey an old-fashioned setting by letting the reader know that the conductor wore a long, double-breasted frock coat. On the same page, I mention the conductor's mutton-chops, his pocket watch and the scent of burning oil and hot iron. With these few words, I hope I have conveyed the fact that *Outlaw's Fortune* takes place over one hundred years ago.

When you write your cross-genre novel, remember to make your setting as important as your character and your plot.

MOOD

Mood, or tone, is another technique that should be considered when setting your private eye character in a cross-genre novel. Previously, I mentioned *Alien Nation: Extreme Prejudice*, and used a scene at the breakfast table to illustrate the importance of character and setting. It is also a good example of using a humorous scene to offset the overall darker tone of the novel. Later in the same chapter, FBI agents meet with Sikes and Francisco at the same hotel breakfast table and discuss the fact that terrorists want their demands met or they will kill one Newcomer a day.

The tone of your novel is an individual choice. The straight PI novel tends to be dark and action-oriented, focusing on the solving of the crime. However, when you plunk your private eye in a setting different from the usual PI haunts, your character doesn't have to be the traditional loner of the straight PI genre.

On the other hand, it is fun to play with the traditional loner image in an interesting setting. Take *Mickey Spillane's Mike Danger*, for example. OK, it's a comic book, but the premise is entertaining: What if Mike Danger (the comic book prototype for Spillane's Mike Hammer) were transported from the 1950s to a politically correct future? Max Allan Collins, the *Mike Danger* writer, has fun with the series, keeping the serious tone of the typical private eye character, but surrounding him with unusual characters. One of those characters is a hologram of his secretary and longtime girlfriend, Holly Graham. Danger can see her, talk to her, investigate his cases with her by his side, but he can never touch, smell or kiss her. It makes for some very interesting plot lines that could never, set in present day, be done.

CHARACTER

The type of private eye character you choose for your cross-genre novel is central to the story. Although Jefferson Birch is a private investigator, he lives in the 1870s west, and my novels have a strong traditional western flavor to them. Birch has a tragic past—a wife and baby who died while he was away working with the Texas Rangers on a case—and even though there was nothing he could have done to prevent their deaths, he still feels that he should have been there to save his family.

In the first book, *Rogue's Gold,* Birch has just met Meg, the owner of a saloon in Grant's Pass in Oregon Territory, and he finds himself attracted to her:

> He couldn't take his eyes off of her and this made him feel uneasy. She was the first woman to get his attention since Audrey died two years ago. That sudden hollow feeling surfaced inside him again when he thought about his wife's death. If she and their child had lived, his son would be two years old now. He poured himself a third shot of bourbon.

If Birch were a present-day private eye, his wife might still have died in childbirth, but the scene would have involved doctors and hospitals and a sterile environment. Instead, I mention in a later scene that Audrey died at home on their ranch with a midwife attending. The mortality rate was far greater back in the 1870s for both mother and child, unlike today with all the miracle drugs and surgical skills available.

In P.N. Elrod's *Bloodlist,* the main character, Jack Fleming, is a newsman in the 1940s who becomes a vampire. Early in the book, he goes back to the family farm in Ohio where he grew up to bring some dirt back to his new home. He visits his grandfather's grave and is overwhelmed by memories of the first time he witnessed death. His grandfather, Grampy, explains that the puppy's death is like the changing of the seasons—death is like winter. Not much later, young Fleming has to deal with yet another death:

> "I think winter is coming," [Grampy] said, and winked at me. It was only September; I didn't understand. I did the next morning when we found he'd died in his sleep. I was the only one who didn't cry at his funeral.
>
> I couldn't help but think of my own change. "What would you think of me now, Grampy?" I whispered at the stone.

Irony is a great plot device—standing over his grandfather's grave, Fleming realizes that he can never die naturally now that he is a vampire.

Always keep in mind that a private eye with a flaw makes the character stand out from the crowd. The nice thing about writing cross-genre is that you can play with it a little bit, as in the case of Jack Fleming, vampire news reporter.

NOW WHAT?

You've created an interesting setting, a mood or tone for your character, and an unforgettable private eye character. Now what? Write your story. Keep in mind the fact that you're trying to balance a plot between two genres. Mix and match; see what you come up with.

Stay true to your story—don't throw too many elements into the plot. You want your cross-genre story to be interesting, not confusing. A reader shouldn't have to work too hard at understanding a cross-genre plot.

Don't try to please everyone. Readers tend to stick to a favorite genre and you can't please a crowd that isn't willing to try something a little different. But for some readers, to find a book that has a mix of their favorite genres is a delightful change of pace. They'll come back for more.

I wrote my Birch series primarily for western readers, and I kept that in mind as I was writing. But I also hoped to draw in some of the mystery crowd. I joined mystery writers' organizations in an effort to get the word out about my cross-genre books. When one of my books was published, I would do local book signings and mailings to libraries and bookstores. All of this work paid off. Eventually, my series caught the eye of Jon Breen, the *Ellery Queen* review columnist, and he wrote very kind reviews of my last two series books—ironically, the two with the least amount of mystery in them.

In the last few years, cross-genre novels have become more popular. My books came along at a time when the attitude toward cross-genre books was changing and they were becoming an increasingly accepted part of the publishing world.

Editors have stopped worrying about the marketing and publicity people, who have stopped worrying about whether the sales reps will be able to sell the bookstore managers on these books. And the bookstore managers? They've realized that they can double-shelve a cross-genre and get double the return by getting the attention of those readers who read in more than one genre.

Writing a cross-genre novel is a good way to combine two of your interests. And a good PI character can be paired with just about any other genre: horror, romance, science fiction or fantasy. Of course, trying to maintain a balanced story is difficult, but if you can dovetail the three elements that create good storytelling—character, setting and plot—your cross-genre novel will be easier to sell to an editor.

The Visual Eyes

Writing Private Eye Comic Books

Max Allan Collins

espite the fact that the *D* in DC Comics stands for "detective," dating to one of that pioneering company's earliest and most successful titles, *Detective Comics* (still running and one of Batman's several homes), the private eye has never made much of a mark in the world of comic books—or, for that matter, comic strips.

The market for detective material in the world of syndicated comic strips is so limited as to be nonexistent, and we won't discuss it in any depth. Suffice it so say that for the fifteen years I wrote the *Dick Tracy* comic strip, I was well aware that if the feature were a brand-new strip, we would never have been able to sell it to subscribing newspapers. Humor forced adventure out a long time ago—decades ago—and continuity strips are dinosaurs. Is *Rip Kirby* still running? That strip, created by the great Alex Raymond, is probably as successful a PI comic strip as was ever created—and Rip hardly became a household name.

Comic books, however, have been home to a number of private eye series . . . though none terribly successful. An early inhabitant of DC's *Detective* comics was Slam Bradley, whose young creators Jerry Siegel and Joe Schuster went on to create another character—maybe you've heard of it—Superman. The popularity of such costumed heroes continues to this day, and science fiction and fantasy—with their possibilities for stimulating visuals—have always been far more popular genres than mysteries in comic books.

Only a handful of private eyes have made any mark at

all in the world of comic books—Pete Marisi's Mike Hammer imitation, *Johnny Dynamite*, in the fifties; writer Joe Gill and artist Giordano's *Sarge Steel* in the sixties; Nick Cuti's *Mike Mauser* in the sixties and seventies. But these were all relatively minor entries in the marketplace, however entertaining they might have been.

Artist Terry Beatty and I created *Ms. Tree*, a tough, female PI, in 1980, predating the prose wave of female private eyes (with the exception of Marcia Muller's Sharon McCone.) The character has enjoyed the longest run of any comic book PI, chalking up over sixty issues and still occasionally appearing as a one-shot or miniseries from DC. But we make no claims for great success; *Ms. Tree* was (and is) a cult favorite, and if Hollywood hadn't optioned the property a few times, it probably would have faded entirely by now. Terry and I have worked on two other PI projects, a four-issue miniseries reviving Morisi's *Johnny Dynamite* (for Dark Horse Comics), and *Mike Danger* (for Big Entertainment), a science-fiction-tinged reworking of Mickey Spillane's Mike Hammer prototype. (Significantly, Mickey couldn't make Mike Danger fly as a comic book in the late forties and wound up doing Mike Hammer as a book character instead.)

The most popular private-eye-style comic book of recent years has been Frank Miller's Spillane homage, *Sin City*, but its sales have been modest in comparison to Miller's superhero work, like the wildly successful Batman graphic novel, *Dark Knight*.

All of this serves as a caveat. The private eye genre—while mainstream in such media as short stories, novels, television, movies and even plays (*City of Angels*)—remains a cult item in the world of comics. Now and then a one-shot appears—Jim Steranko's handsome *Chandler*, for instance, or the recent limited-edition adaption of *The Little Sister*—but no mainstream successes come to mind.

There may be some logical reasons for this lack of widespread success. The private eye story, no matter how much hard-hitting action and sizzling sex it might occasionally contain, is primarily a literate, intellectual type of story. Cerebral, even. In a search for truth, the private eye moves from suspect to suspect, carrying out interrogations that do not necessarily lend themselves to wild, stimulating visuals. Film *noir* effects sometimes used in comic books, such as moody "lighting" and odd "camera" angles, can only go so far.

If you are foolish enough to attempt a private eye story in so unfriendly a marketplace, here are a few tips and how-to's.

There is no set format for comic book scripting, although you may be able to acquire some sample scripts to give you *some* idea of an acceptable format by writing a query to a comic book company. In general, remember to break down the script (and it's very much a script, in the movie or play sense) by pages, and each page by panels. You need to at least suggest, by way of your panels, the design of the page; you needn't be terribly specific, because the final design is the artist's job (and you will usually have separate pencillers and inkers, so really it's the *pencillers'* job). Each panel consists of a description of the action and any dialogue. My way of doing this is of my own devising, but here is an example of a sample page (from *Johnny Dynamite—Underworld #1*):

PAGE TWENTY-FIVE
Row One
PANEL ONE—His sportscoat off, Johnny has pulled over beside the road in the desert. He has opened the trunk and is looking down into it where he (and we) see a wide-eyed, terrified, mussed-up Freddie Faust, stuffed in there, on his back, looking up, hanky stuffed in his mouth, hands bound behind him.

Johnny: He sold you *out*, Freddie. Tony sold you out. He *told* me. I *know* you pulled the trigger . . .

PANEL TWO—Johnny has helped Freddie out; they stand behind the rear of the car now, in desert setting, Freddie (hands lashed behind him with belt) with his back to Johnny who trains .45 in gloved hand on the hood's back. Faust no longer has hanky in mouth, now—he looks very worried. Johnny has the smallest, nastiest of smiles.

Johnny: You boss is *dead*, now. It'll be a closed-casket service, though . . . unless they pop *glass* eyes in for the ones I shot out.

Row Two
PANEL THREE—Sweating in fear and from the heat, Faust glances back at off-camera Johnny in this close-up or medium close-up, pleading, worried.

Faust: Johnny . . . Dynamite . . . you *know* how it works . . . I just did what he told me to do. It was nothin' *personal* . . . I *liked* that kid. She was sweet. But if it wasn't me, it woulda been some *other* button.

PANEL FOUR—A very frightened Freddie glances back as Johnny is right behind him with the .45 shoved in his back; Dynamite is as cold as the day is hot.

Johnny: Tony told me different. Tony said you was following your *own* initiative. Don't matter. Either way, you gotta *die*, Freddie.

Row Three
PANEL FIVE—Longish shot as Freddie stumbles along while Johnny walks behind him with .45 in hand. In the desert.

Faust: Where in the hell we *goin'*?

Johnny: No *special* place in hell. This'll do—turn around, Freddie . . .

PANEL SIX—A bright sun shines over a sand dune. The dialogue is caption floats.

Johnny: See, I promised Selma the guy who killed her would die *slow*. And since I'm not quite sure if there's *really* a hell in the hereafter . . . fact, I'm not sure there's a hereafter at *all* . . .

Again, this is only how I set up my script pages, and it's a format I invented, not industry standard (there isn't one).

You may notice, from this sample, that I often use a traditional PI first person narration, in captions, to give a more literary flavor and tie in my comics to the style of the classic private eye novels of Chandler, Spillane, Ross Macdonald and others.

Note, too, that the setting—in this case, a desert—has some visual sizzle (literary). The dark alleys of urban settings are also good, but many detective stories have scene after scene in offices, apartments, mansions or private homes and you have to minimize these in comics, or devise something inherently, visually interesting about those mundane settings.

One of the requirements—whether drawback or not, I'll leave to you—of doing a private eye story in an *ongoing* comic book (either a monthly title, like *Mike Danger*, or a miniseries, like *Johnny Dynamite*) is that each issue must have some action. This is not a rule, but a convention; however, I promise that any editor you manage to convince to do a private eye comic book will, before long, be reminding you that you are attempting to attract that wide, superhero-numbed audience, and an all-talking-heads, no-fight-scene, no-sex-scene issue will be met with editorial dismay and disdain.

Despite the discouraging things I've said, crime and private eye comics have made a modest comeback, and while the private eye may not be a "natural" for this medium, it can be done. You just have to blunder into the darkened room like any good PI, and hope not to get sapped.

Humor in the Private Eye Novel

Parnell Hall

I am somewhat reluctant to discuss humor in the private eye novel because funny is supposedly the kiss of death in publishing. I remember when my first book was published I got reviews referring to it as hilarious, so I went to my publisher and asked him why he wasn't advertising the book as funny. He said, "Shhh! Funny doesn't sell. Suspense sells." If you look at the covers of my old private eye novels it says right on the front of the dust jacket, "A Stanley Hastings Novel of Suspense."

I am also reluctant to discuss the humorous private eye novel because humor is so hard to define. Indeed, analyzing what makes things funny can reduce even the wittiest and most articulate person into an incoherent, blithering fool.

Worse than that, it is boring.

Jokes are funny. Explaining why they are is dry, tedious and pedantic. Anyone attempting to do so would probably risk harming his or her career.

Fortunately, no one reads my books anyway, so I am free to take a shot.

What makes a joke funny?

In Simon Brett's *A Comedian Dies*, the comedian sidesteps that tricky question by firing back the one-liner, "An audience laughing at it."

Exactly. And this would be an excellent example, if it weren't for the fact that *A Comedian Dies* wasn't a private eye novel. But you get the idea. We all know *when* something is funny. *Why* it is funny is another matter.

Since I have already admitted to reviews characterizing

my books as humorous private eye novels, I might as well discuss them. Particularly since I don't set out to write comedy. At least not caper comedy as in "let's take a funny premise and see what we can do with it." I am writing murder mysteries, and any humor is incidental to that.

But where does the humor come from?

To begin with, I am writing a private eye novel. Like many private eye writers, I am writing in the first person. So the narrative is, of course, colored by the character of the narrator.

My detective, Stanley Hastings, is a failed actor/writer. As such, he often treats his narrative in the nature of a performance, so his observations take on a humorous bent sometimes bordering on stand-up comedy routines. For instance, in the book *Shot* he turns on the Jay Leno show and observes, "First up was Armand Assante, which is one of those names that sounds more like a crime than a person. 'You are charged with armand assante in the first degree, how do you plead?' 'Not guilty, your Honor.' (The charge was later plea bargained down to a misdemeanor charge of patty hearst.)"

A bad joke? Undoubtedly. Yet memorable. I've had people inquire years after the fact, "Say, what was that Armand Assante bit in one of your books?"

While it is not that remarkable a joke, it is the type I find I can get away with. Particularly since I am the first to admit that these are not terrific jokes. For instance, in that same book *Shot* I have Stanley observe, after some wisecrack or another, "Unfortunately, like most of my jokes, it is the type that amuses only me, which is probably one of the reasons I never made it as a writer."

If this makes no sense to you, please remember what I said at the beginning about discussing humor making one sound like a blithering fool.

But where was I? Oh, yes, humor. Well, let's take the bull by the horns and make a statement.

Humor arises from two fundamental sources: situation and character.

We are all familiar with the *sit*-com. It is a funny premise that can be stretched out for thirty minutes, including commercials, and can be stated simply and succinctly in a single sentence for inclusion in *TV Guide*.

Since I've already stated I don't write that type of private eye novel, the humor in my books must come from the *character*. Which is a rather ticklish point with me. Because, like many private eye writers, I based the character of my protagonist somewhat loosely on myself. So to read reviews about Stanley being a fumbling, bumbling private eye, comically stumbling his way through another case, does not gladden my heart. Particularly since I see him as a smarter, braver, more resourceful and ingenious version of me.

Which I actually do. And which is a bit confusing. If I see him as clever, but others see him as inept, where do they get that impression?

The answer is television.

Stanley Hastings is not a TV detective. He's the type of detective that exists in real life. I know, because for two years I did his job. And it is the contrast between the glamorous TV supercop and an ordinary person attempting to fill the role that creates the impression of ineptitude on the one hand, and humor on the other. Particularly since Stanley's self-deprecating nature is such that he is often the one making the comparison and finding himself deficient. He will say, for instance, in his narration, "In the movies, detectives have a set of skeleton keys or know how to pick a lock. Failing that, they kick the door down. I have none of those talents. If a door is locked, I can't get in."

People find this funny on the one hand, but classify Stanley as a bungler for admitting it on the other. I disagree. I think he's a real-life person, and if he's constantly being tripped up by life, I think that's because that's what life constantly does.

I also think the ingenuity he shows getting in the door is far more interesting than if he's been able to just go "click."

But the main thing is, if life keeps giving him a pie in the face, it isn't because he incompetent. That's just life.

I hope this has been some help in shedding some light on humor in the private eye novel.

Of course, I don't really know.

I don't write humor.

I write suspense.

FROM THE EDITOR'S DESK

So You're Gonna Walk the Mean Streets

Michael Seidman

As an editor, the first question I usually ask writers is why they're doing what they're doing. Sometimes it's in terms of why they're writing at all; sometimes it is a question as to why they've chosen a particular form or genre or topic. "Having to write" is not enough; it's simply obsessive behavior and there are drugs that'll help you control the urge so you can get on with your life. It reassures me when the person with whom I'm speaking says they're writing because they have something to say. (Entertainment is an acceptable answer, too; it just isn't enough for me.)

You're contemplating walking the mean streets of PI fiction. Why? What is it about the category, this sometimes honored, sometimes maligned subset of the mystery genre, that has drawn you?

Most of the successful writers in the field are tilling that soil because they grew up reading the so-called standards in the form. Depending on your age, that could mean following the adventures of Race Williams or Phillip Marlowe; Sam Spade or Mike Hammer; Shell Scott or Honey West; Nero Wolfe or Travis McGee; Miles Jacoby or Alo Nudger; Sharon McCone or . . . Sherlock Holmes. The better writers have read them all, good, bad or indifferent. And that's the first thing you have to do if you are serious about pursuing a career on the mean streets: know the background, know what's been done, know what works and why, and know what you like and what you want to accomplish.

Here's a little background, then, some of the basics. A taste, really, because the history of the category is traced elsewhere in these pages.

THE CHANGING PI

Sherlock Holmes was very much a private eye: Not an employee of a recognized, state-run law enforcement agency, he accepted fees from clients who needed his assistance in solving crimes that had touched their lives. He had a love/hate relationship with the police, in the form of Inspector Lestrade of Scotland Yard, and failure wasn't an option. He had honor. The line to today's private investigators is as straight as railroad tracks. With a curve every now and then.

Beginning in the late twenties, the PI began to take on not only that hardboiled aspect that came to define the writings, but a distinctly American tone. That grew through Raymond Chandler and Dashiell Hammett's work, to Ross Macdonald's, and to today, with such standard names as Muller and Grafton and Paretsky and Powell, with detectives named Sharon, Kinsey, Vic[toria] and Phoebe.

And, as we moved further from the world wars and Depression, other changes became clear. The investigator moved from being a solo act, a veteran who'd seen too much blood on the soil of Europe or in the Pacific, who carried a load of angst that could keep a school of psychology or a cafe table of existentialists busy for an eon or two; the PI went from being a tough-on-the-outside, soft-on-the-inside male (somewhat paralleling the hooker with the heart of gold, who often played a role in the tales) to a woman with the same nature. And into the future.

Independent (but with contacts in the right places), honorable (but willing to stretch a point in service of the client) and determined (sometimes to the exclusion of having a life outside of the investigation), the PI came to represent some kind of

American ideal: She or he is a hero.

In the late seventies, Marcia Muller introduced Sharon McCone; shortly thereafter, Sue Grafton and Sara Paretsky published their first Kinsey Millhone and V.I. Warshawski novels, and the face of the fiction began wearing a lot more makeup. Coupled with the formation of Sisters-in-Crime, women began to dominate crime fiction generally, representing a true demographic: More women buy books and they wanted fiction that spoke to them. (This is something that's happening to some degree in all forms of fiction. In the summer of 1996, the editor of a highly respected literary magazine said that white males were facing a real crunch when it came to having their work accepted. There are, naturally, some nasty jokes about the situation, related by white males in bars, which is where they seem to be able to still find acceptance.)

QUALITY SELLS

All of this is said to serve as a reminder to you—or to anyone getting ready to take the plunge into the cold waters of writing for money—that things are always changing in terms of the definition of a genre or form. The iconography may remain the same, but social influences cannot be denied or ignored; the constant (we hope) is going to be good writing.

As happens whenever a category gets "hot," publishers and writers rush to feed the flames. Unfortunately, the readers become aware of the fact that just because a book seems to be something they want to read (because of packaging, labels, etc.) doesn't mean that it is worth reading. They start to shy away from new releases (unless there is a great word-of-mouth push), publishers tell their editors that the category isn't selling, something else moves to the top and a new category is hot, publishers and writers rush to . . . The wheel keeps on turning.

The bandwagons continue to roll, and the writers who define the new and continue to succeed at the old are the ones who write better, who push the envelope, who are willing to take risks. The writers satisfied to do what's been done and continue copying what's gone before keep shifting gears and, at least to this editor and reader, produce a cotton candy fiction that satisfies for the moment (if it doesn't give one a stomach-ache), serving up lots of empty calories. The choice is yours. As an editor who may have to consider your work at some future date, however, I'm going to let you know what I'm looking for, what it is that makes a book work for me. While my tastes differ from those of other editors (as theirs differs from each other, as well), keep this one thought in mind: We all recognize better writing, and with shrinking lists and markets, better writing is going to win out every time.

First—and quickly—research. Some has to be done because the laws governing the actions of a private investigator vary from state to state. Know the law. Several years ago, as a judge in the Private Eye Writers of America Best Paperback category, I received a novel set in New York. The setting, the ambience, was trite but otherwise acceptable: a standard, 1940s office in Times Square, black-edged gilt letters on pebbled glass; there may even have been a swinging gate in the office. You've seen this setting hundreds of times, usually in black and white. I never got into the office, however: The lettering on the door announced the PI's name, followed by the words "Private Detective." In New York, detective is a police rank and cannot be used by an investigator in the public sector. If that very basic fact was wrong, what else was going to be, and how much of that would I not recognize? Suspension of disbelief was not only lost but shattered and there was no reason to keep reading. The novel didn't make my final cut . . . nor the nomination list of any other judges. (It's another example of the bad driving out the good—we'd have all been better off if the book hadn't been published at all. Except for the writer, of course, who did get the one advance. I don't recall seeing another by that author.)

FIRST STEPS

Knowing what you have to know, then, let's begin with the creation of a novel. The novel, all novels, are about people and the events that occur in their lives. Big, small, meaningful or banal, things happen to people and better writers begin with the people. So, who is your private investigator going to be?

Where does he or she come from, psychologically as well as historically? Why has this person opted to follow a career path that usually isn't one to warm the cockles of a mother's heart? What is it about this person that will make the people with whom he comes in contact talk to him? What is it about him that will drive people to confess? All too often, clues are offered because the book would stop dead if they weren't, but there's nothing about the detective that is compelling enough to cause me to even talk to the person, much less offer the information requested and required.

One of the major differences between characters that go on in long-lived series and those consigned to the remainder tables early on is that of the full-dimension portrait: a depiction that lets the reader recognize and accept the "hero" as someone not only viable, but capable. You cannot offer your reader that kind of character unless you know the character intimately, so your task is to create a full biography, something that offers the background, training, skills (professional and human) and emotional makeup that would be found in someone doing what your character is doing. It is not sufficient to start layering in the details later, when something is called for and the character must perform in a particular way. If, as a reader, I'm not able to accept an action based on the character I've been following, I lose faith. Having lost faith, I lose interest. Having lost interest, I consign your book either to the shelf or, professionally and much worse, to the reject pile.

Everything must be in place well before the action is called for. If it isn't, you're going to have to either begin again or create a different action based on the "reality" of the character and the story you are telling. This is true of each and every player in your story (and it doesn't matter one whit what kind of story you are telling; we're dealing with universals here). Don't begin your thought with the idea of the crime or anything else: Begin with fully realized characters and let them move and be moved by the events you are relating. It makes everything more natural, keeps the suspension of disbelief in force, and makes motives and methods things the reader will accept easily, rather than requiring us to make allowances for the story.

With your characters in hand—at least the central ones and definitely the continuing ones, and ninety-nine times out of a hundred, you are going to be creating a series because that is what publishers and readers are looking for—you are ready to move to the next step: what you are going to do with them. The story, as we said, is about the characters, so what happens to them?

CREATING THE STORY

That's where the outline comes in. Now, don't start cringing and whining about how an outline "locks" you into something, how it is restrictive and keeps you from telling your story properly, and how you are more comfortable just winging it because you have the idea of what you want to tell the reader in your head. The truth of the matter is that an outline is not a blueprint, which requires an architect to follow it line for line or the building will collapse. No, the outline is a road map, offering the driver the option of any number of alternate routes, as long as there's some destination in mind. You can get off the road whenever you want to, stop at some local sight worth seeing, and then keep going; you can turn off and take a back road rather than a superhighway; you can even switch directions now and then . . . as long as you know where you want to wind up.

Who will your victim be? What will have happened to him? How has it happened? When (and is the time important)? Where did it occur? Who called your investigator in and what makes her suitable to the job? (Just because someone has a job description doesn't perforce mean that they are capable of all aspects of that job; ask any of your writer friends about the editor who frustrated them.) When do they get called into the case; and if it is an active police investigation, what's their excuse for becoming involved and how are they going to deal with the fact that they're not supposed to do things like that? Why does the PI do the things she will do that will bring about a solution?

REMEMBER THE IMPACT

All too often in crime fiction, the victim is a puzzle piece and the point is to fit that piece into the finished picture. The events of the story have no lasting (or even, strangely enough) passing impact on the characters. Unless the relatives of the victim are carved of glacial ice, the murder of Grandpa means (or should mean) more than a momentary sadness. Ask the survivors of a crime how their lives change. How many times have you read a PI novel in which, say, a daughter hires a detective, is filled with sadness at the murder of the father, but evidences nothing that indicates any feeling whatsoever . . . except, perhaps for the eye, with whom she eventually falls into bed?

The survivors are rarely the same after the event and one of your functions as a novelist is to explicate those changes. Murder mysteries are not about puzzles; they are about tragic events in the lives of a group of people. Your private investigator may not be a psychologist (though he or she may have to know psychology) on the scene to help the victims overcome, but the PI should recognize the weight of the event.

Police officers develop a *galgenhumor*, a gallows humor, that allows them to handle what they see and have to deal with. If your detective is at the crime scene, then, how are you going to have him react? Is that reaction in keeping with the background you've created? If this is the first corpse he's had to deal with, and it is ripe with age (or a crispy or a floater), what's going to happen? Sure, he's tough (or, at least, medium-boiled; beta males just don't hack it), but still . . . Oh, your PI's a woman? Fine, how is she going to react, then? Has she had experience with corpses? If you present her as being tough as nails, is she going to be someone the reader wants to spend time with? If she falls to pieces, displays a clichéd hysteria (clichéd, but, well, I've had the misfortune of having to deal with situations like that, and throwing up seems the most logical thing to do), will we have faith in her abilities?

The reaction doesn't have to be shown at the moment. Maybe your PI is musing alone (over bourbon and/or Perrier) or talking to an associate—at some point, show us the reactions, the effect.

Every action has an opposite but equal reaction. That's a law of physics and it should be a law of writing. If you are going to follow a time-honored tradition and set up a police officer as an ongoing antagonist, how are your PI's actions going to affect her? What is she going to do? Is it reasonable? Is it "right" in terms of how people in authority deal with others? Characters, like people, have a psychology that drives them and any investigation pushes buttons. As you begin driving the road that's going to bring your investigator to the solution, consider the side roads of emotion that are going to be passed. Is the husband of the victim going to be a suspect? Of course he will; he's a prime suspect just about every time. How is he going to react? Will those reactions serve to make him more suspect or less? Is he a red herring?

Who, what, when, where, how, to what effect: They are the key elements to your outline, the basis of your novel; and they are questions that cannot be answered until you know who your characters are so you know how they will react. The two pieces, then, the characters and the outline, go hand-in-glove with telling your story. Having solved the puzzle of those elements, it's time to go on to the next step.

POINT OF VIEW

By tradition (again) the private eye novel is told in first person. It needn't be done that way, but the point of view is immediately recognized by your readers and your readers, by and large, want the comfort of familiarity.

In first person, there is no knowledge unless the PI discovers it in full view of the reader. Another aspect of the fiction, something shared with the cozy and virtually all other satisfying mystery reads, is the fair play concept. It is simple, really: The reader must be in a position to solve the crime, to have an equal opportunity. It is a game between the author and the reader. All the clues must be present; the trick is to lead the reader into believing one thing, then have the detective show an alternate version that's the correct solution. Some seemingly minor clue makes the difference.

The clue, however, has to be one to which the reader is privy. The detective, in first person, cannot receive information that the reader doesn't have, because we are with the detective all the time. You cannot get away with revealing a clue at the end, based on a phone call the detective received when we weren't there.

Because we are with your hero all the time, the first person voice adds an immediacy to the action; we are in the event with her, seeing through her eyes, hearing what she hears. How we interpret that input is up to us, the readers, and makes the difference in our being able to arrive at the solution.

You will not be rejected (by editors or readers) for telling your story in third person . . . just a little more quickly compared to other writers in the form. Since I have no objection to my writers (or my own writing) being judged on its own merits, rather than against some arbitrary paradigm put in place by often tired traditions, I can easily suggest that you try third person if it appeals to you. That appeal, again, will be surrounded by the reasons you've chosen the PI form: if what appeals is the tradition, the voice of Chandler, Macdonald and Hammett (the old tripartite god of the hardboiled), that's the way you're going to write, the type of character you're going to create. If it's at the altar of Muller, Grafton and Paretsky that you worship, your work will be informed by them. (And they, while creating new traditions, have made honorable use of the old.)

The urgent matter is that you find the voice that's most comfortable for you as a storyteller. Editors can tell when a writer is simply aping what's gone before in the belief that it's what's going to sell, and when the manuscript offers the freshness of a new imagination. Those editors, if you listen to them at conferences, are always looking for that something new and different, even if our lists don't always show the evidence of those statements. The final decision, as always, is yours.

In third person, we are not with the detective at all times, and may become privy to conversations and events they may not witness. If the information is important, at some point the investigator has to be made privy to it. Things are not as immediate, because we receive information through the filter of the author, and some things are repeated so that everyone is playing with the same deck by the end of the story. However, the same rules apply: The reader must have all the clues and they must all contribute either to solving the case or misdirecting the reader.

Also traditional in the PI form is a cynical humor and a use of metaphor and simile. To my mind, those are aspects of a writers' view of the world and ability as a wordsmith.

There is nothing more jarring than humor that isn't funny or a metaphor that is less than apt. So, unless you have the particular word skills necessary to express your detective's vision that way, don't. Stick to what you know and what you can do, and do it as best you can. Simply because something worked in the past doesn't mean that it will continue to; because someone is able to do something doesn't mean that you can. Keep dancin' with what brought ya.

CLUES ARE IN THE DETAILS

Just as when we watch a magician, the reader wants to be fooled; that's the point of the game we're playing with each other. So, your solution should be a surprise, forcing the reader to go back and find the clue that he or she missed, even though it was in plain sight. As you present the information needed to bust the perp, don't surround it with Day-Glo circles or point neon arrows at the facts. Information can and should be presented in casual conversation as well as interrogation; it is not mused upon by the detective or anyone else; it is simply there for the taking by the reader clever enough to notice it.

Clues are not simply relayed in verbal information; they are present in the physicality of persons and places, and that can make description a key element.

You want your novel to move forward; you want to keep the reader turning pages and moving toward the end. Every time you stop to slather description onto the story, you are stopping the motion; therefore, keep in mind that everything doesn't have to be presented at once.

When you meet someone, are you immediately aware of everything that makes them up physically? When someone enters a room, can you tell from your seat in the far corner what color eyes they have? Whether their roots are dyed? Can you see the wart between the pinky and ring finger? Of course not. So don't stop your ongoing action to present a pore-by-pore, cell-by-cell description of your characters, even your new ones. Let the information come out bit by bit, to both your detective and your reader, in the way it actually does. Mention the eyes when your detective is talking directly to the character; have the wart noticed when they shake hands or when the character lights a cigarette, or whenever it is likely such a feature would be seen. If you're dealing with a clue, make the mention casual; simply saying her unusually blue eyes sparkled brightly in the light of the hundred-bulb crystal chandelier could be a setup for later revealing that she was wearing contact lenses. (I don't know that contact lenses would have that effect. If I were using this as a clue in a story, I'd have to find out how colored lenses would appear in that kind of light.) I've also added a bit of description of the room in which the characters are playing out this part of the story. Of course, you would notice a fixture like that immediately upon entering a room, but what about the subtle pattern in the weave in the upholstery of the couch? Does it make a difference? Is it a clue or a way of speaking to the wealth and taste of the person who owns the furniture? Is that the clue?

TALK SOUP

I guess you can always have the detective and owner discuss it. That brings us to dialogue, an aspect of writing that many experts consider the most difficult, because it isn't easy to make it sound natural. Natural does not mean quoting conversations verbatim. You don't want to fill the pages of your manuscript with the uhs, umms, likes and you-knows that account for most of what seems to be said nowadays. Think of it this way: The most effective dialogue doesn't consist necessarily of what is said, but of what is heard. That is what you want your reader to be aware of and you can use excess verbiage as a way to bury the important information. If all conversations are just two talking heads yammering away, the reader is going to lose interest.

While it is true that unless someone is giving a speech, we tend to speak in a series of shorter sentences with lots of breaks and interruptions, there are times when one of your characters may have to go on longer than "natural." By natural, I mean opposed to conversation that is furiously paced, a quick back-and-forth. Whatever is happening, if you watch people in conversation, you'll notice that they don't just talk. There are motions: facial tics, movements of the hands, eyes scouting for a way out or the next person to talk to. Add those elements to your novel: Break up the words with action, and the action with words.

Actions and words: Let the words your characters speak and their actions (slamming a water glass onto a table, caressing a cheek) indicate the way in which the dialogue is delivered. Don't fall prey to the easy way out—a series of boring and laughable dialogue tags and adverbs. If I can't tell whether a line is being delivered humorously or angrily, your telling me that it's so won't make it any more clear or believable to me. There may be times when it is necessary, but it should never be necessary more than two or three times in a novel of 70,000 words.

Characters say or ask, just as you and I do; *said* and *asked* are invisible on the pages and soundless in the reader's head.

I rarely "declare," infrequently "observe," never "muse" . . . the list of such "said" book-isms is endless and their use annoying. Read a page of dialogue on which every comment is followed by some carefully chosen alternative to "said" and you'll start laughing. Unless the book is a comedy, that probably isn't the reaction the writer hoped for. Indeed, if there are only two people speaking, you probably don't need more than the opening and closing quotation marks to indicate all the reader needs. If you do, look to your characters and what is being said—the fault, dear Horatio, lies with them.

Finally, this remains to be said: The private investigator has often been compared to a knight riding in quest of the Grail of Justice and Truth. The comparison is apt, and while the PI as antihero is not unheard of, the popularity of the *character*, the reason the eye has survived all the changes of taste dictated by a changing society, is that the character fulfills a special need in all of us: a wish for someone not with superhuman powers, but with just the abilities we wish we had in the schoolyards and mean streets of our childhoods and adult days. Someone to confront the bullies and keep us safe.

You will, I hope, having read this, continue to write your story in the way that is right for you. All the rules, dictated either by what has gone before or by what any one person wants to see, are nothing more than a record of what's been done and what might be done as seen by a particular sensibility. What gives your work value is that it is a record of your particular sensibility.

Down these mean streets a writer must go, alone and unafraid. That is, after all, one of the reasons you're writing, isn't it?

Printout to Published

Michael Seidman

nce your manuscript is completed, the hard work begins: getting published. You'll try to find an agent, of course, but that isn't always possible. And it is not *impossible* to find a publisher who will consider your work even if you are unagented. Networking at conferences, writing letters, making phone calls—whatever seems the most likely approach for you should be followed, with the less likely approach reserved for use immediately thereafter. The idea is to get your manuscript into the hands of an editor, the person who may buy your book.

After an editor receives the manuscript, regardless of how it gets to the desk, the process is the same. It begins with reading, and making the first determination: Do I need this book for my list?

Just because a house publishes mysteries doesn't guarantee you a slot . . . even if you're good. Some houses don't do certain types of fiction (you'll have to examine catalogues and the bookshelves to make that determination); in other instances, an editor may have too many books of the kind you've written both in inventory and scheduled for the future. There may be a sense on the part of the marketing department that your particular subgenre is not selling well right now. The editor may have a stomachache. Or be over budget (which can cause stomachaches as well as pains in other parts of the anatomy).

SELLING THE BOOK TO THE PUBLISHER

If the editor is enjoying the read, other factors are being considered: How much editorial work is necessary? How will I package it? Do I know of any titles that might compete too directly (that is, is it too derivative)?

Having decided, finally, that the book is something he wants to acquire, the editor begins one of the more tedious parts of the process: developing a profit and loss statement for the proposed book. Everything has to be factored into the equation—the estimated sales (based on the editor's knowledge of the market, previous sales results and your track record, if any); the estimated length; the cost of typesetting, printing, binding, cover art, lettering, promotion, publicity and advertising (usually a set figure assigned to books of the type); cost of sales; estimated cost of royalties (they are a business expense); and, yes, the advance you are going to receive as well as the editor's salary (and the salaries of all the other people involved in getting your book from manuscript to the shelves; overhead is a major factor in figuring costs and may account for up to 50 percent of the estimated profits).

With the profit and loss statement in hand, and with a firm idea of how you're going to fit, some editors are forced into editorial meetings. There, with the marketing department, financial and editorial executives, and other editors waiting, your editor explains why your book is special, why it is worth the investment of time, money and energy that's required. He or she may, for instance, have to defend the decision to acquire the book to a subsidiary rights director, who will be interested in the possibilities of selling rights to paperback houses or overseas, and who might point out that paperback houses are no longer interested in female private investigators, unless they have a love life. (I'm not saying that's the case, just offering it as an example.)

Finally, an OK is given. Everyone in the publishing house is now aware of the book, of the fact that it is going to be on the list, and what actions are going to be necessary. Of course, the editor still has to negotiate for the rights, and either you or your agent may not be satisfied with the offer. An agent is not going to automatically guarantee you a larger advance. He or she may have more leverage than and unrepresented writer, but that's it. The major difference in the negotiation is going to be in the area of subsidiary rights, where your agent will want to maintain control of foreign, motion picture and electronic rights, among others. You, as an individual, are not in a position to negotiate those rights, and an editor dealing directly with you will try to keep them for the house. You might, as a counter to that, request that those rights revert to you after the book has been in print for a year. If you've obtained an agent by then, that representative will be able to use the rights, perhaps. If you haven't, it doesn't make all that much difference. And if the publisher has sold the rights, you'll have made more money, though not necessarily as much as you would have if your agent sold the rights. The publisher will undoubtedly take 50 percent, an agent only fifteen or twenty.

THE EDITING PROCESS

The editing process differs from editor to editor. Some are active, changing words and sentences and dialogue; others suggest the changes to you. Few editors will rewrite completely. If there's a new character needed, or a substantial change, you'll be told about it and it will be up to you to make those changes as quickly as possible. In most instances, you won't get the second half of your advance until the changes are accepted. It is also more likely than not that if major changes are needed, they will be requested before the contract is offered. Editors are willing to discuss the changes, and most are reasonable. However, if there comes a point at which neither you nor the editor is going to budge, you can either swallow your pride or return the advance. Every contract makes it clear that "acceptable" will be defined by the publisher.

After the book is edited and copyedited, you should have the chance to look it over. If your contract doesn't require it of you, check with your editor. You want to see the changes that have been made and, when the copyeditor is as good as most that I've worked with, there'll be questions for you about meaning, about facts. Everything comes under the copyeditor's purview and their function in our lives is to save us from embarrassment. When you have the copyedited manuscript in hand, read it carefully, answer any queries put to you, discuss with your editor anything that bothers you, and get the manuscript back to the publisher in the allotted time. Once a book is in production, you don't want to do anything that will delay the publication date.

POST-EDITORIAL STAGES

It's a sure bet that you're not going to have the opportunity to design your own cover. Covers are one of the marketing tools, and the publishers have a pretty good idea of what is going to sell for them. The editor has discussed certain concepts with the art director; the art director has talked to the artist; everyone has consulted with marketing and, sometimes, with booksellers. Quite often, of course, that means your jacket will look just like every other jacket; in other cases, rare but not unheard of, you won't have any idea at all of what your editor might have been thinking about when the art was approved. There are times when someone is going to take a risk with your book. Keep in mind that the chances being taken are part of a strategy that, the publishers hope, will result in your book being noticed . . . to the detriment of the book next to it.

You are going to be asked, at some point early on, to fill out a questionnaire or two. These are for publicity purposes and really are quite helpful, even if publishers aren't always successful in getting you the attention you'd like. You'll be asked for information about your background, contacts in the local media, and anything else that can be exploited to promote your book. If you have any ideas that might generate publicity or promotional possibilities, now is the time to mention them. Don't be disappointed if the company publicist doesn't start jumping up and down immediately; only rarely can anything be done before the book is in galleys.

Galleys are a stage of production between initial typesetting and printing. Galleys are uncorrected, and this is when you're called upon to contribute again . . . or should be. At this time you have an opportunity to proofread the book before it goes to print. If you ignore the chance, or if you don't take it seriously, you cannot blame the publisher for any errors that appear. Yes, the publisher is going to have someone (or maybe two) doing proofreading as well, but it is your book and you want to maintain as much control as you can.

By this time you may have been shown some sketches of proposed cover art. This is a courtesy, and only that. While an editor might, on occasion, approach you for input—especially if there's a need for special information—generally the cover art is a marketing tool, and the publisher will do what it wants to do.

The same applies to the flap and jacket copy: In some houses the editors write it, in others there are copywriters. Years of experience have taught them what has to be done and how. They know not to give away crucial clues; they know how to grab an audience. It is possible, though unlikely, that if you're an advertising executive your input will be sought. Again, what you may find cute or otherwise interesting doesn't necessarily work in the marketplace . . . and that's where everything is put to the test, including your book.

One of the things your editor has been doing is preparing catalog copy and other information for the sales reps. There will be tip sheets, keynote lines (a sentence or two that will allow the rep to present the book quickly and succinctly), and whatever other items a particular house uses. Everything is gathered—including the sales representative—and the presentations begin.

SELLING THE BOOK TO THE PUBLIC

It is a sad but true fact: Almost no one between the editor and the first readers of the finished book care very much about the story you've told—unless you have, in some way, broken new ground. The sales reps certainly don't want to be bothered.

They are, after all, hearing about anywhere from fifty to several hundred new titles. They're not going to remember the details of the plot, or much of anything else. What they want to hear from the editors and others talking about the books are the few words they can use most effectively to present the titles to their accounts. The most important information is the genre or subgenre in which you are writing, where you live and what your track record, if any, might be.

They will look at the cover art, consider it in terms of all the other books out there (the cover is nothing more or less than a billboard, competing for the customer's attention against the hundreds of other books released into the same market-place), might suggest changes, may applaud, and then will turn to the next book on the list.

Although it sounds as if you're getting short shrift, the unvarnished truth is that more often than not, the rep doesn't have much more than thirty seconds to present each book to the buyer at any given store. The buyer wants to know where you live (if you are local, that can be a selling point), what you've done in the past (to check the store's records to see how you've sold there) and perhaps whether your character is going to continue in a series. And he will compare your cover art to what's been seen from other publishers for that season. And that is about it! They don't want to hear about your novel being the best book ever (they've heard it too often); they don't want to know about the clever plot twists (they'll read the book in galleys and decide for themselves how clever you are); all they want are the bare facts and basics.

Once the orders start coming in from the field, the publisher can begin to estimate, with a sense of reality, how many copies to print. Most publishers don't set the final print order until the key accounts have arrived. These include orders from the chains (Borders, B. Dalton, Barnes & Noble, etc.), and those wholesalers (most particularly for paperbacks) and jobbers who represent fixed percentages of annual business for the publisher. With those figures in hand, the publisher can estimate how many copies will be needed, because it is already known that they generally account for a certain percentage of a book's sales.

Publishers can, and occasionally do, try forcing the numbers a little. They offer incentives to a bookseller, in the form of discounts or free books with orders for a certain number, or make any kind of deal that makes business sense, so as to push orders up. A book that can't be seen can't be bought, and publishers do want those books out there . . . otherwise there'd be no point in publishing them.

What a publisher can't do (or at least shouldn't), and so what an editor can't do, is lie. If an editor overhypes a book at a sales conference, and if the reps then overhype, and if the book doesn't do as well as expected, the editor and the rep will no longer be believed. Rather than the boy who cried "wolf," we're dealing with the publisher who cries "great." Eventually, neither of them are believed, and it can take a long time to regain the faith of the book buyers (or sales reps).

REVIEWS

The most effective sales tools are pre-pub reviews, those in *Publishers Weekly*, *Booklist*, *Library Journal* and other trade magazines. Booksellers, librarians and movie production offices read the journals, see what's getting the good reviews and order accordingly. It doesn't always work out. (The only guarantee is that your editor is waiting for the next book. Maybe.) But the reviews can generate enough interest to guarantee good intial orders. The books, because they will be available in quantity, will be visible in the stores. The bookstore owner has an interest in moving stock; the customers have a perception of lots of interest in the book (otherwise, there wouldn't be so many copies available), and interest is generated. Those early reviews, combined with good word-of-mouth about your book, are the most effective promotion tool available.

They are also effective selling tools for the publisher. If you've sold your novel as a hardcover original, those reviews and the sales and the buzz on the streets and in the mystery community combine to make the paperback houses take an interest in your work. That, in turn, generates more income: There's the additional advance you receive, there's the additional royalties, there's increased attention (so your value goes up to everyone involved) and, if the paperback edition of an earlier book arrives shortly before a new hardcover from you, they serve to boost sales for each other. It's an ideal situation; unfortunately, it doesn't always happen.

AFTER PUBLICATION

And that's what we sit down to consider, about a year after publication date: What, exactly, happened? Why did the book do better or worse than expected? Was it the cover? How can we get more reviews next time? What can we do to make things better (no matter how well they went) for the next book?

Publishers are committed to their writers; it is a relationship that takes it for granted that we're in this thing together. Your book wasn't acquired simply because you're a nice person. The editor had reason to believe that you were a worthwhile investment. While we may smile about it, editors do resent the way authors are jumping from house to house these days, chasing the buck. There's nothing that can be done about it, but the fact remains that when we buy a manuscript, we are thinking in terms of a long run together. It is over time that a successful writing career is established. While there are writers who rocket to the top, the reason we hear so much about them is that they're so rare; they are the exceptions.

Publishing is a business (even if an editor's job is to spend a lifetime drawing to an inside straight—the idea is to stack the deck now and then). It takes considered risks and looks for a profit. Writers, too, must look at what they do as a business. The more you know about what the publishers are doing, the better able you will be to negotiate with them, deal with them and produce a product that they can turn into their own; you are creating a raw material for another industry, and we need each other.

You are going to hear horror stories galore; many of them are undoubtedly rooted in truth. You will hear stories of wonderful success; some of them, too, are absolutely true. Don't take either as the absolute truth, however. They are aspects of the same thing.

The only guarantee you can count on is this: It doesn't matter what the trends are, what fad is current, which genre is "hot." What matters is that you write better than the author of the manuscripts on either side of yours in the pile. If you do, you will be noticed—and being noticed is where it all began . . . with your manuscript open on my desk.

CONTRIBUTORS

LAWRENCE BLOCK is the author of the Burglar series and the Matt Scudder series. He has won the PWA Shamus Award twice for Best PI Novel and twice for Best PI Short Story, all with entries in the Scudder series. He is a past president of PWA and a frequent contributor to *Writer's Digest* magazine.

MAX ALLAN COLLINS has earned an unprecentended seven PWA Shamus award nominations for his Nathan Heller historical thrillers, winning twice with *True Detective* in 1983 and *Stolen Away* in 1991. The newest Heller is *Damned in Paradise* (Dutton, 1996).

CATHERINE DAIN is the author of the Freddie O'Neal PI series, for which she has been nominated twice for Shamus awards for Best Paperback PI Novel.

WILLIAM L. DEANDREA is a two-time winner of the MWA Edgar Award. He passed away during preparation of this book and will be missed.

LOREN D. ESTLEMAN is not a past officer of PWA because he refuses to run. He has, however, been nominated for the Shamus award three times for Best Novel—winning once with *Sugartown* (Houghton, Mifflin, 1984)—and an amazing ten times for short story, winning twice.

ED GORMAN is the author of the Jack Dwyer PI series and of recent thrillers of *The Marilyn Tapes* (TOR, 1994) and *The First Lady* (TOR, 1995). Two of his short stories are currently in production as motion pictures. He is the publisher and co-founder of *Mystery Scene* magazine.

SUE GRAFTON is the author of the bestselling Kinsey Millhone series, the most recent of which is *"M" Is for Malice*. She has won the Best PI Novel Shamus award an unprecedented three times, with *"B"*, *"G"* and *"K"*. She is a past president of PWA.

JAN GRAPE'S short fiction has appeared in *Deadly Allies* and *Deadly Allies II*, *Lethal Ladies* and *Lethal Ladies II*, many Cat Crimes anthologies, and numerous other anthologies and magazines. She is a past vice-president of PWA and editor of the PWA newsletter *Reflections in a Private Eye*.

PARNELL HALL is the author of the Stanley Hastings series. His novel *Movie* (Mysterious Press, 1995) was nominated for a Shamus for Best PI Novel of 1995. He is a past president of PWA.

GAR ANTHONY HAYWOOD has won the Shamus Award twice, for Best First PI novel and Best PI Short Story. He is currently writing for the TV series *New York Undercover*. He is the author of the Loudermilk and Aaron Gunner series. He is the second winner, after Les Roberts, of the PWA/St. Martin's Press Best First Private Eye Novel contest, with the Aaron Gunner novel *Fear of the Dark* (St. Martin's Press, 1988).

JEREMIAH HEALY is a past president of PWA. He is the author of the John Francis Cuddy series. His Cuddy novel *The Staked Goat* won the Shamus Award for Best PI Novel. His most recent Cuddy novel is *Invasion of Privacy* (Pocket Books, 1996).

JERRY KENEALLY is a real private eye and the author of the Nick Polo series. His most recent novel, however, is the thriller *The Conductor* (Signet, 1996). He is a past vice-president of PWA.

WENDI LEE is the author of the Jefferson Birch western PI series and the Angela Matelli contemporary PI series. Her most recent Matelli novel is *Missing Eden* (St. Martin's Press, 1996).

JOHN LUTZ is the author of the Nudger and Carver series. His most recent novels are *Lightning* (Holt, 1996), featuring Carver, and *The Ex* (Kensington, 1996), which was also a major motion picture. He won the Shamus Award for Best PI Novel with his Carver novel *Kiss* (Holt, 1988). He is also the author of *SWF Seeks Same* (St. Martin's Press, 1990), which was made into the motion picture *Single, White Female*. He is a past president of both PWA and MWA.

CHRISTINE MATTHEWS'S short fiction has appeared in *Ellery Queen's Mystery Magazine*, *Deadly Allies* and *Deadly Allies II*, *Lethal Ladies*, *Cat Crimes Takes a Holiday* and Mickey Spillane's *Vengeance Is Hers*. She is the co-editor of *Lethal Ladies II* and, with Robert J. Randisi, is author of the upcoming mystery novel *Murder Is the Deal of the Day* (St. Martin's Press, 1997), which introduces amateur detectives Gil and Claire Hunt.

ROBERT J. RANDISI is the founder of the Private Eye Writers of America and creator of the Shamus Award. He is the current president of PWA, having been railroaded into the job by acclamation by former president Parnell Hall. It is his first time in that office. He is the author of the Henry Po, Nick Delvecchio and Miles Jacoby PI series. His most recent novel, however, is a thriller called *In the Shadow of the Arch* (St. Martin's Press, 1997). He is the editor of fourteen anthologies and, with Ed Gorman, founder of *Mystery Scene* magazine.

LES ROBERTS is the author of the Saxon and Milan Jacovich series. He won the first PWA/St. Martin's Press First Private Eye Novel Contest in 1986 with his Saxon novel *An Infinite Number of Monkeys* (St. Martins Press, 1987). His most recent effort is the Milan Jacovich novel *Collision Bend* (St. Martin's Press, 1996). His Jacovich novel *The Lake Effect* (St. Martin's Press, 1994) was nominated for Best PI Novel.

MICHAEL SEIDMAN has been a mystery editor for thirty years. Among the writers he has "discovered" and published are Teri White, Sean Flannery, Robert J. Randisi, Sandra West Prowell, Neil Albert, Alan Russell, Thomas D. Davis, G.M. Ford and Richard Barre. All have been nominated and/or have won Edgar and Shamus awards, the most recent being *The Innocents*

(Walker & Co., 1995) by Richard Barre. He is a frequent lecturer and instructor on the subject of mystery writing and has authored two books on the subject, *From Printout to Published* and *Living the Dream*. He has also published short fiction and has been a frequent contributor to *Writer's Digest* magazine.

INDEX

More Great Books for Writers!

Missing Persons: A Writer's Guide to Finding the Lost, the Abducted and the Escaped—Now your characters can go beyond the phone book to search for missing relatives, old friends and vanishing villains! Professional PI, Fay Faron, shows you why people turn up missing and the search procedures used to find them.
#10511/$16.99/272 pages/paperback/available September 1997

Murder One: A Writer's Guide to Homicide—Build believable homicide scenarios— from accidental murders to crimes of passion. Prosecuting investigators Mauro Corvasce and Joseph Paglino take you step by step through motives, weapons and disposals of bodies—illustrated with scene-by-scene accounts from real life cases.
#10498/$16.99/240 pages/paperback/available September 1997

The Writer's Complete Crime Reference Book—Now completely revised and updated! Incredible encyclopedia of hard-to-find facts about the ways of criminals and cops, prosecutors and defenders, victims and juries—everything the crime and mystery writer needs is at your fingertips. *#10371/$19.99/304 pages*

Amateur Detectives: A Writer's Guide to How Private Citizens Solve Criminal Cases—Make your amateur-crime-solver novels and stories accurate and convincing! You'll investigate what jobs work well with sleuthing, information-gathering methods, the law as it relates to amateur investigators and more!
#10487/$16.99/240 pages/paperback

Body Trauma: A Writer's Guide to Wounds and Injuries—Bring realism to your work using this detailed examination of serious bodily injury. You'll learn what happens to organs and bones maimed by accident or intent—from the 4 steps in trauma care to the "dirty dozen" dreadful—but survivable—chest injuries.
#10488/$16.99/240 pages/20 b&w illus./paperback

Writing Mysteries: A Handbook by the Mystery Writers of America—Sue Grafton weaves the experience of today's top mystery authors into a mystery writing "how-to." You'll learn how to create great mystery, including making stories more taut, more immediate and more fraught with tension. *#10286/$18.99/208 pages*

Scene of the Crime: A Writer's Guide to Crime-Scene Investigations—Save time with this quick reference book! You'll find loads of facts and details on how police scour crime scenes for telltale clues. *#10319/$15.99/240 pages/paperback*

Police Procedural: A Writer's Guide to the Police and How They Work—Learn how police officers work, when they work, what they wear, who they report to and how they go about controlling and investigating crime. *#10374/$16.99/272 pages/paperback*

Modus Operandi: A Writer's Guide to How Criminals Work—From murder to arson to prostitution, two seasoned detectives show you how to create masterful crimes while still dropping enough clues to let the good guys catch the bad guys.
#10414/$16.99/224 pages/paperback

Mystery Writer's Sourcebook: Where to Sell Your Manuscripts—Part market guide, part writing guide, this is an invaluable companion for all mystery, suspense and crime writers. You'll discover in-depth market reports on 120 mystery book and magazine publishers, techniques from top writers and editors and 125 agents who represent mystery writers. *#10455/$19.99/475 pages*

Private Eyes: A Writer's Guide to Private Investigators—How do people become investigators? What procedures do they use? What tricks/tactics do they use? This guide gives you the "inside scoop" on the world of private eyes!
#10373/$15.99/208 pages/paperback

Deadly Doses: A Writer's Guide to Poisons—This comprehensive reference book addresses the crucial issues you'll encounter when "poisoning off" a character.
#10177/$16.99/298 pages/paperback

Armed & Dangerous: A Writer's Guide to Weapons—You'll learn how to arm your characters with weapons to perfectly suit their crime. Hundreds of examples and easy-to-understand language make complicated details completely accessible. *#10176/$15.99/186 pages/paperback*

Writing the Modern Mystery—If you're guilty of plot, character and construction murder, let this guide show you how to write tightly crafted, salable mysteries that will appeal to today's editors and readers. *#10290/$14.99/224 pages/paperback*

Malicious Intent: A Writer's Guide to How Criminals Think—Create unforgettable villains with the help of this guide to criminal psychology. You'll explore the fact and fiction of who these people are, why they commit their crimes, how they choose their victims and more! *#10413/$16.99/240 pages/paperback*

Cause of Death: A Writer's Guide to Death, Murder & Forensic Medicine—Discover how to accurately "kill-off" your characters as you are led step by step through the process of trauma, death and burial. *#10318/$16.99/240 pages/paperback*

The Writer's Essential Desk Reference—Get quick, complete, accurate answers to your important writing questions with this companion volume to *Writer's Market*. You'll cover all aspects of the business side of writing—from information on the World Wide Web and other research sites to opportunities with writers' workshops and the basics on taxes and health insurance. *#10485/$24.99/384 pages*

Writing and Selling Your Novel—Write publishable fiction from start to finish with expert advice from professional novelist Jack Bickham! You'll learn how to develop effective work habits, refine your fiction writing technique, and revise and tailor your novels for tightly targeted markets. *#10509/$17.99/208 pages*

Conflict, Action & Suspense—Discover how to grab your reader with an action-packed beginning, build the suspense throughout your story and bring it all to a fever pitch through powerful, gripping conflict. *#10396/$15.99/176 pages*

Voice & Style—Discover how to create character and story voices! You'll learn to write with a spellbinding narrative voice, create original character voices, write dialogue that conveys personality, control tone of voice to create mood and make the story's voices harmonize into a solid style. *#10452/$15.99/176 pages*

The Writer's Digest Sourcebook for Building Believable Characters—Create unforgettable characters as you "attend" a roundtable where six novelists reveal their approaches to characterization. You'll probe your characters' backgrounds, beliefs and desires with a fill-in-the-blanks questionnaire. And a thesaurus of characteristics will help you develop the many other features no character should be without. *#10463/$17.99/288 pages*

How to Write Attention-Grabbing Query & Cover Letters—Use the secrets Wood reveals to write queries perfectly tailored, too good to turn down! In this guidebook, you will discover why boldness beats blandness in queries every time, ten basics you *must* have in your article queries, ten query blunders that can destroy publication chances and much more. *#10462/$17.99/208 pages*